A Pinch of This, A Handful of That

A Pinch of This, A Handful of That

Rushina Munshaw-Ghildiyal

westland ltd
61 Silverline, Alapakkam Main Road, Maduravoyal, Chennai 600095
No. 38/10 (New No.5), Raghava Nagar, New Timber Yard Layout, Bangalore 560 026
93, 1st floor, Sham Lal Road, Daryaganj, New Delhi 110002

First published in India by westland ltd, 2013

Copyright © Rushina Munshaw Ghildiyal, 2013

Photography: Mrigank Sharma, India Sutra
Food Styling: Rushina Munshaw Ghildiyal

All rights reserved

10 9 8 7 6 5 4 3 2 1

ISBN: 978-93-83260-58-4

Designed by: Kavita Chopra Dikshit (Red Design Company)

Printed at Repro India Ltd., Mumbai

This book is sold subject to the condition that it shall not by way of trade or otherwise, be lent, resold, hired out, circulated, and no reproduction in any form, in whole or in part (except for brief quotations in critical articles or reviews) may be made without written permission of the publishers.

In memory of those who have left me to wherever they may be — they will always dwell in my heart. We do not have to rely upon memories to recapture the spirit of those we have loved and lost they live within our souls in some perfect sanctuary which even death cannot destroy.

From *The Thoughts of Nanushka; Vol VII to XII* — Nan Witcomb

~ my grandparents Mulraj Kapadia, BC Munshaw and Kapilaben Munshaw.

~ my grandparents-in-law S.S. Raturi and Mohini Raturi.

~ my darling, darling dad Hamir B. Munshaw and my father-in-law, Ratnambar Datt Ghildiyal — I will never stop missing you both. We hope you are up there with Alex and Nonie sharing a beer and cheering your grandchildren in whom we see both of you!

~ my older brothers Hasit and Ashu Munshaw — losing each of you has left a hole in my life. Ashu Bhai — you were the brother of my adult years. I wish you had lived to see this book published.

~ Garry Craft, kindred spirit, we'll meet again, don't know where, don't know when, some sunny day.

CONTENTS

Foreword by Sanjeev Kapoor | *page x*

Why I Cook | *page xii*

Cha ke Coffee? | *page 1*
Chai goes beyond being simply a cuppa in India; its robust, hot, spicy sweetness personifies the country. As universal as Chai is in India, it is also intensely personal, because there are as many recipes for tea as there are people in India.

Ketchup Hota Kaddu Bhara | *page 7*
Moti Mummy's kitchen coloured my growing-up years; and her legacy to me, has been her love for preserving and pickling.

Chak Chak | *page 27*
Nani provisioned and ran a kitchen the old way but she also moved with the times and embraced new influences to cater to her family's desires and requirements. This sense of culinary adventure is her legacy to me.

Spice of Life | *page 53*
Of all the women in my life my mother has been the strongest influence on my cooking. And the singular quality I am proud to have inherited from her, is her ability to reinvent herself into the cook, the person she is cooking for, needs her to be.

Lost Recipes | *page 75*
If the women in my life set the bar on home cooking, my father was responsible for introducing my palate to all sorts of flavours I would

never have tasted at home.

Maharaj | page 91

Our cook at home, Maharaj was not a culinary teacher in the direct sense, but a lot of the dishes I crave — and have learnt to cook as a result of those cravings — are ones he cooked and were, in essence my first introduction to them.

Discovering the Kitchen | page 109

Most of the cooking I did when I was growing up was hobby cooking, and I think it made a big difference to the future cook I would be. I wonder if I would have developed as adventurous an attitude to cooking if I had been trained in traditional cooking at that point.

The First Dance | page 137

After I got married, I slowly learned to cook for two. I also learned tips and tricks from women around me at work and on the trains home that optimized time and allowed me to cook quickly and efficiently, but keeping the meals nutritionally balanced.

Yummy Mummy aka Chief Cook, Espionage Agent | page 177

My two kids have helped me master the art of disguising vegetables so I can smuggle them into their food. Also, the art of of giving dishes innovative names: Monster Blood for one!

India on My Plate | page 199

It would take a lifetime and many meals to just complete sampling one's way through the vastness of Indian Cuisine! Thankfully however, I live in Mumbai, a metropolis that has a signature menu of its own.

Culinary Souvenirs | page 225

The best way to discover a place is through its food. Culinary souvenirs is a term I coined encompass all these little pieces of my holidays attached to the memory of great dining experiences.

A Perfect Bite | *page 251*
When I eat, I need to get all the elements on my plate perfectly balanced in each bite. Not only am I obsessed with getting the perfect bite, it is a hobby to create A Perfect Bite of a dish with an ingredient.

Kuch Meetha Ho Jaaye | *page 285*
Whatever is offered, sweetening the mouth is a quintessential tradition that the women in the house carry forward.

In Gratitude | *page 301*

Index of Recipes | *page 307*

Foreword

Food lovers flock together. And so do those who convert their love and passion for perfected recipes into cookbooks. All through my many, many years of researching and authoring cookbooks on various topics, I had not come across one on food memories like this one till Rushina announced her new project, a collection of recipes she inherited as a legacy from the women in her life, aptly titled *A Pinch of this, A Handful of That*.

Well, this book is a bonus for those who celebrate food and for those who write as prolifically as Rushina Munshaw Ghildiyal does. Her life and style are all headed in one direction — right into the kitchen! My association with Rushina goes back many years and we interact on many issues related to all things food. I find her blogs brilliant and her new venture APB Cook Studio is a pioneering initiative taken by a genuine foodie who will do justice to it.

A Pinch of this, A Handful of That is a memoir with recipes, recollecting Rushina's growing up years in Mumbai and collating the many influences on her palate by the women in her life. It is enriched with colourful personal anecdotes, recipes from home cooks of various communities, and Rushina's own creations from a wide variety of influences. Gujarati undhiyu, Sindhi curry, aubergines in sweet and sour sauce, curry leaf fish, butter tava prawns — a variety of dishes have become part of a colourful whole that is the menu in her kitchen today.

Sharing experiences is a very giving process, and Rushina has laid her heart out, all for the love of food and preserving her culinary inheritance. I would urge the brand new cooks, the budding ones, the expert cooks, the old hands as they say, to try the recipes from *A Pinch of this, A Handful of That* and be transported to whatever culinary adventure the food so passionately described wants us to enjoy.

If we ever got science to get us a cookbook that would give the aroma of the recipe one is reading, I would most definitely put this work in the priority list. Because good food always smells so divine that the taste buds clamour for it with impatience. I wish Rushina good luck for this book, and also for all the forthcoming ones! We share a passion for food and love for our culinary inheritance that has so many tales to narrate.

SANJEEV KAPOOR

Why I Cook

This book was conceived in half an hour. Nobody is born cooking; I certainly wasn't. And if you consider a week's worth of meals from my kitchen you will be hard put to find any pattern; Monday could be a simple Sindhi curry with rice, Tuesday rice paper rolls and glass noodle salad, Wednesday could be homemade garlic pasta, Thursday might be my signature dumpling soup and Friday could be rajma chawal and raita. There is no method to this madness —meals from my kitchen happen as a result of what is available in season, dishes that have passed the family test but mostly owing to my whims. And one day I found myself wondering, where did these whims come from? What made me the cook I am?

As I mused to myself, I realised that I have a food memory associated with every event and every person in my life! And that this activity I love so much — that I spend more than half my waking hours indulging in — is a result of my idiosyncratic personal history. This book is an exploration of my journey to being the cook I am today.

India is ancient, with a culture that is centuries old. But very little of it is documented, especially when it comes to our cuisine. What is documented is the equivalent of a pinch of salt compared to what is available. And all the rest is a living legacy handed down orally from one generation of women to the next.

Even today in most Indian families, women and cooking are inextricably linked. Somewhere in our childhood, we women naturally shoulder our mothers' responsibilities, watching, helping in the kitchen and imbibing their culinary knowledge. Eventually becoming food providers of our own families. The most significant influence on my cooking then, has to be from the women in my life. The roots of my cooking are an inheritance from them, a culinary legacy. My earliest memories are of their voices, telling me things about food. In spite of never really entering the kitchen as a young girl, somehow their kitchen secrets filtered down to me and, when required, came to the fore to become the heart of my cooking

And in this also lies the evolution of home cooking. The quintessentially Indian inheritance of parents from the different culinary heritages is something many of us will identify with. And the blending of those cultures in the cooks of the following generations. The ethos of my cuisine is rooted in the culinary influences of my grandmothers' kitchens, a blend of two dialects, Kutchi and Amdavadi of the regional cuisine of Gujarat. It is not even so much the things I learned that amaze me, but the way I learned them. It was completely subconscious!

Today if I discard sprigs with flowers on them when I clean coriander, it is because my grandmother did that in the belief that they caused rifts in the family. If I always add salt to a dish with my left hand, it is because my sister-in-law once told me that adding salt with the left hand meant one would never over salt a dish. And if I never taste food to check if it is done, relying instead on my eyes and nose to guide me, it is because I saw all the women in my family do that. Tasting food was disrespecting those you were cooking for.

Somewhere in my early teens, I began to watch, help and imbibe. Cooking was a fun activity to indulge in when I wanted to play grown-up or impress the adults. And when the time came to exchange the dolls' houses and cooking sets of childhood for the real thing, it all began as an adventure as I experimented with being the decision-maker of my own kitchen but the honeymoon ended and it became more trial than pleasure. I changed from a career woman to a stay-at-home mom and went through a period in which I came to hate cooking. Daily meals of RDBS (roti-dal-bhat-subzi) became routine and I was loath to cook!

But my grandmothers, mother and mother-in-law came to guide me. These women who had gone before me had catered to large joint families through good times and bad. And even in times of strife, family dinners had the makings for 'The Big Fat Indian Family' type of movie where every one of those sixteen or more people at the table would find something in the meal that they liked! I realised that beyond the procurement, planning and preparation, they could keep track of an entire family's likes and dislikes. For women of our grandmothers' generation planning a meal went beyond throwing a few things together; everything from the season (winter, monsoon or summer), the last two meals (to avoid repetition) and individual preferences of each member of the family were taken into account. I used to marvel at this ability till I watched my friend Mita mentally planning meals while shopping at a supermarket. Women today perform the same equations — only the backdrop is different. Heightened awareness led to more observation and I discovered that I was not alone! Women everywhere faced the same question I did every day. What to cook?

My kitchen window faces a bank of kitchens in the building across the road. And every day an orchestra of cooking plays out in front of me! It starts with a Maharashtrian lady on the fourth floor cooking the evening meal for her family and continues when a young lady on the second floor puts off the flame under the meal she is cooking for her family's tiffin the next morning.

Curiosity about what others were cooking led to discussions with women everywhere; other mothers and grandmothers I met when I took my son down to play or waited outside his school. Talking about food became a great way to break the ice. And the rewards were fantastic. Occasionally, it would be an interesting new recipe I would hastily scribble on the nearest scrap of paper. Sometimes, I would be honoured with a cooking demonstration. I learned to think creatively with what I had on hand in my kitchen. And along the way, I made friends. That's when food became a language for me. A language that opened up new doors. I found that whenever I took that first step towards a stranger and spoke in the language of food, the rewards were delicious! Cooking became a way of loving. And with time I thrived on preparing exotic, fantastic meals. I also discovered a whole new cuisine from my husband's community, which in turn opened my palate to the variety of community cuisines we have in India, specifically Mumbai.

And then I got really lucky in finding a career to legitimise what had become my obsession with food! As I wrote my first words as a food writer, the aspect of food and food ways and their ability to evolve through successive generations of women fascinated me; and no city offered richer pickings for this than the home kitchens of Mumbai.

If the women in my life initially influenced me, it is this city that shaped the cook I am today. While Mumbai has a very dynamic dining scene, the most interesting facet of her cuisine-scape seldom gets its due — the versatility of her community kitchens. And while the chefs of Mumbai's restaurants are often lauded, the real cooks of this city, the women whose hands feed this city, seldom get any recognition.

You only have to walk through a residential colony to get a whiff of the rich offerings there. The aromas that float on the sultry evening breeze are legion! Maharashtrian phodnis crackle in one home, Bengali mustard fish simmers in another, here a south Indian sambhar bubbles away while a Punjabi tadka crackles there! In Mumbai, food has a way of crossing the divides of community, caste, religion and region, resulting in a variety of cuisines, aromas, flavours and tastes combining into one huge melting pot.

This book is a celebration of the inextricable link between food and women. A secondary but no less important objective, is to document and preserve. That said, it is not meant to be an encyclopaedia — for that is what documenting Mumbai's home cooking would require — but to offer a taste of the fabulous food culture and culinary history of which I have been the recipient. I am aware that there are many things missing and several recipes you might have wanted, but the rule of thumb I followed was that if the recipe made it past the test of a busy schedule that juggled home, career, kids and energy levels, it was a recipe worth sharing. Any gaps are purely my fault, as are any errors. Of course it would be doing the male species an injustice to disregard their contribution to the culinary legacy that is passed on. Men also play a large part from kings and conquerors who entered India, to their cooks and khansamas who stirred in their own culinary touches to the evolution of Indian cuisines. On the home front they is often the defining factor in what is cooked in the kitchens. My grandfathers and father made an equally large contribution to the cook I am today. If the women in our house laid the foundation of my palate, it was my father who expanded it. And today I am lucky to have an understanding, supportive husband, who shares kitchen duty with me. Our food choices are often based on what we can cook together.

Finally, I would simply like to say that a cook is a condiment in themselves, so in this book I give you a life's worth of recipes with happy memories. They are only mine till you cook them; then they become yours. With a pinch of this and a handful of that.

Rushina Munshaw Ghildiyal

Cha ke Coffee?

Because in India, Everything Starts and Ends with a Cup of Tea!

Like everything in the kitchen was India, my first foray into to cook chai. Yes, cook! Because cha, the traditional masala chai drunk by Gujaratis, is far from a delicately brewed tea; in fact Gujarati masala chai is a bracing, robust beverage that is boiled for a good few minutes and is strongly fortified with a special spice mix called cha no masalo (chai masala).

Afternoon tea was a daily ritual in our home. The preparation of chai was a duty usually carried out by the youngest daughter-in-law present. However, that day, by popular consensus, it was decreed that I would make the tea (I was eleven or twelve years old then). It was a rare moment when I had my mother, who was guiding me, to myself and I revelled in it. Every nuance of the afternoon is etched clear in my mind. My mother's soft hands guiding my smaller ones as I measured out the ingredients; her voice as she listed ingredients and proportions, steadying me as I grasped the heavy tapeli (pot), holding me back so I wouldn't singe my nose on its hot edges, looking in and helping me carry the heavy tea tray to my waiting family. But most of all I think I remember her proud smile as I basked in the glow of everyone's praise.

I ended up marrying into a Garhwali family and have never made chai for them — not the Gujarati way at any rate, because they prefer their tea the 'English' way, with a little milk stirred in after the tea has brewed. But it is in this difference that I learned just what 'chai' means to India. As universal as chai is in India, it is also intensely personal, because there are as many recipes for tea as there are people in India.

Moti Mummy's Chai Masala House Blend

We usually make a batch of chai masala and store it in an airtight jar to last a couple of months. This mix is good for relieving the aches and pains of colds, coughs, flu and fevers. It is also handy to add to puddings, cakes and other baked goodies. I even add it to chikoo milkshake where it offsets the caramel sweetness of the fruit.

Time: 30 minutes | Makes 600 gms of masala

Ingredients
- 200 gms dried ginger
- 200 gms green cardamoms pods
- 100 gms whole black peppercorns
- 50 gms cloves
- 50 gms cinnamon
- 2 pieces of nutmeg
- 8 bay leaves

Method
- Dry all the ingredients in the sun or in the oven at a low temperature for 2 hours to ensure no moisture is left in them or the masala will spoil.
- Grind each spice individually in a dry grinder or coffee grinder.
- Sift the ground spices through a fine sieve and grind the larger pieces left in the sieve again.
- Combine all the powdered spices and mix well.
- Transfer to an airtight jar to store.

Munshaw House Chai

On days when life gets a little difficult to handle and I want a cup of comfort, I go back to the way masala chai was made in my mother's house.

Time: 10 minutes | Serves 4

Ingredients

- 2 cups milk
- 1-2 lemongrass leaves, cut into segments
- 10-12 mint leaves
- 4 tsp sugar or to taste (optional)
- ¼ tsp chai masala powder or to taste (page 2)
- 4 green cardamom pods, pounded
- ½" piece of fresh ginger, coarsely crushed
- 4 tsp tea leaves

Method

- Combine the milk with 2 cups of water in a pan deep enough to prevent boiling over.
- Add the remaining ingredients, except the tea leaves and bring to a boil.
- Lower the heat and add the tea leaves. Be careful, because when the tea leaves go in, the concoction tends to rise and can overflow.
- Raise the heat and allow to boil. When it boils and rises, lower the heat, till it settles. Raise the heat and allow to rise again, then reduce the heat and leave on simmer.
- When the tea rises again, take the pan off the heat.
- Once it settles, return to heat.
- When it rises again, switch off the heat, strain into cups and serve.

Cutting Chai

It is a temerity to try to teach an Indian how to make chai, but here is a recipe that is the best accompaniment to pakodas.

Time: 10 minutes | Serves 4

Ingredients
- 4 tsp tea leaves
- 3 green cardamom pods
- 1" cinnamon stick
- 2 cloves
- 2 cups milk
- Sugar to taste

Method
- Boil 2 cups of water in tea kettle. Add the tea leaves along with the spices and bring to a simmer.
- Add milk and continue to simmer for a few minutes longer.
- Strain into cups and sweeten to taste.

Suleimani Chai

Suleimani chai is the preferred tea of the Bohri Muslim community and is usually sipped after a heavy meal, such as biryani to aid with digestion.

Time: 15 minutes | Serves 2

Ingredients

- ½ tsp tea leaves or 1 tea bag
- 2 tsp fresh lime juice
- 3 tsp sugar or more to taste

Method

- Bring 2 cups of water to a boil in a pan and turn the heat off.
- Add the tea leaves or tea bag and let it steep for 5 minutes, covered.
- Strain the tea into cups, add lime juice and sugar and serve hot.

Rose And Pistachio Kehwa

This is a delicious dessert tea I developed a few Christmases ago for my hampers. I make the mix in large batches and use as required.

Time: 10 minutes | Serves 1

Ingredients
- 2 tbsp vanilla sugar (or plain sugar and a 1" piece of vanilla pod)
- 1 tsp Turkish rosebud tea or dried rose petals
- 1 tbsp pistachio flakes

Method
- Combine 1 cup of water and the vanilla pod (if using) in a pan on high heat and bring to a boil.
- Remove from heat and stir in the sugar, rosebud tea or petals and pistachio flakes.
- Cover and let it rest for 2 minutes and then savour.

Ketchup Hota Kaddu Bhara

The women of the house were immersed in yet another afternoon of industry. Dozens of glass bottles were being sterilised in a hot bath and added to the crude production line that snaked around the perimeter of the cavernous kitchen. First stopping at the kitchen counter to be filled with hot tomato ketchup, then shuffling along to have a measure of paraffin wax poured into their necks and be sealed with a cork. A quick stop at the kitchen sink to be rinsed off, dried and labelled and finally they went into a carton bound for the kothar or storeroom.

Two days ago, the morning newspaper had announced that tomato prices were at an all-time low. And Moti Mummy, my paternal grandmother, decreed that the ladies of the house would prepare a year's worth of tomato ketchup.

Kapilaben Munshaw or Moti Mummy (elder mother) as we called her, came from Thasra, a small village in Gujarat and brought with her the agrarian culinary legacy she inherited from her mother. She applied that knowledge to living in Mumbai and a large part of it involved an annual cycle of producing food for storage. In the agrarian tradition that most of India follows, Moti Mummy provisioned for the entire year. Tons of grain and pulses would be negotiated for and delivered to our home during the harvest season. Perhaps because of her agrarian origins and also in part to losing her husband early and bringing up her family virtually single-handedly, I remember Moti Mummy as being almost compulsive in her need to store things. And not only were the dry goods stored, but when produce was in season and cheap, marathon sessions would be undertaken: like ketchup-making when tomatoes were cheap or pickling lemons when they were in season.

I do not remember the food that came from Moti Mummy's kitchen as being particularly exceptional, save for a few memorable dishes: seasonal treats like khajur pakoda in the winter, aam ras scooped up with bapada rotis (layered flatbreads) in the mango season, dudhi no halwo, undhiyu and dhakko that induce an almost painful nostalgia for idyllic times. But these were few and far between. Moti Mummy's legacy to me is her love for preserving and pickling. According to family lore, Moti Mummy made about ninety different kinds of pickles every year! I meant to document her recipes,

I really did, but I procrastinated. What can I say? I was young, life stretched ahead — and then one day it was too late. But I remembered some of the pickles that appeared at the table through the season and researched amongst the family to perfect the recipes. Through these I carry forward her legacy every year.

Aam Papad
(Mango Leather)

In the mango season, Moti Mummy would often make aam papad, spreading layers of mango purée on a thali in the hot summer sun, till it dried to a thin elastic film. We would keep asking whether it was done, till the day finally came when we would find her sitting in her favourite corner of the bed, glint in the eye and a secretive smile on the face. She'd pull out the box with a glistening roll of luscious golden-yellow, tangy goodness and divide it into our greedy waiting hands. She made it the traditional way, drying just the pulp in the sun, unlike commercial versions that come with added sugar. I devised an oven version a few years ago.

Time: 10 minutes + drying time | Makes 1-2 discs, 8" wide

Ingredients
- 1 cup mango pulp
- ⅓ tsp ghee

Method
- Process the pulp to a very smooth purée and reserve.
- Spread the ghee over 2 thalis, 8" wide or a large baking sheet.
- Pour the mango pulp on the thali and spread out thinly.
- Cover with a net or muslin cloth and place it in the sun to dry.
- Bring it in at night. Return to sunlight the next day.
- Continue to do this, till it is no longer sticky and has a smooth surface.
- You will know it is ready, when it comes off the thali easily.
- Roll into a cylinder and store in an airtight box.
- Keep for 1 week at ambient temperature in a dark place, 1 month in the refrigerator or 1 year in the freezer.

Handvo
(Gujarati Cuisine's Answer to Meatloaf)

Handvo is a traditional Gujarati savoury cake that is amazingly easy to make and hard to get wrong. I have always likened it to the Western meatloaf in terms of ease of cooking and the protein punch. This was Moti Mummy's favourite snack and often made an appearance at tea time. I remember enjoying the burn of the hot tea after bites of spicy handvo.

Time: 1 hour + overnight for fermentation | Serves 6-8

Ingredients
- 2 cups rice
- 1 cup husked, split pigeon peas (toover/arhar dal)
- ¼ cup husked, split black gram (urad dal)
- ¼ cup husked, split moong beans (moong dal)
- ¼ cup husked, split Bengal gram (chana dal)
- ¼ cup cracked wheat (dalia)
- 1 cup sour natural yoghurt, whisked smooth
- 300 gms bottle gourd (lauki/ghia/doodhi), grated
- 4 tbsp cold-pressed sesame or peanut oil
- Juice of ½ a lime
- 1 tsp sodium bicarbonate
- 2 tbsp sugar
- 1 tsp methia keri sambhar masala (commercial)
- ½ tsp turmeric powder
- 3 tbsp green chilli-ginger paste (see note)
- Salt to taste

Tempering
- 4 tbsp cold-pressed sesame oil
- 2 tsp black mustard seeds
- 2 tsp sesame seeds (til)
- 2 tsp carom seeds (ajwain)
- ½ tsp asafoetida powder (hing)

Method
- Wash the rice and dals and soak them together for 4-5 hours. They are at the right stage for grinding when they swell and crumble on being pressed between the thumb and forefinger. Drain the soaked rice and dals and grind them to a paste. Transfer to a large bowl.
- Add the broken wheat and sour yoghurt and mix well. Cover and leave the batter to ferment overnight.
- The next morning, mix the batter well.
- Add the remaining ingredients, except the tempering. Mix well.
- Pour the resulting batter into a greased baking tin.
- Put the oil for the tempering in a small pan on medium heat. When hot, add the mustard seeds, and then the sesame seeds, carom seeds and asafoetida powder and fry, till the sesame seeds darken to a golden colour. Pour the contents of the pan over the surface of the batter in the tin.
- Place the tin in an oven preheated to 200°C. Bake for 30-35 minutes, till the crust is golden brown. I also sometimes divide the batter into muffin trays and bake it into little savoury cakes. The baking time for smaller cakes reduces to 25-30 minutes, and requires a little more attention.

Notes:
- *To make the green chilli-ginger paste, grind equal quantities of green chilli and ginger to a paste.*
- *Remove the cracked wheat and this recipe becomes gluten-free.*
- *To cut down the cooking time, one can buy ready-made flour mix for handvo.*
- *I also find it convenient to roast larger batches of the grains individually in the proportions above, grind them coarsely, mix and store in an airtight jar. When required, simply spoon out as much as you need.*

Serving suggestions: *Traditionally handvo is served with raw sesame oil, but as kids we often got a little honey or chundo (page 40) to top it with. Coriander chutney also pairs very well with it. Wash it down with masala chaas (page 52).*

Morio
(Spicy, Savoury Yoghurt and Millet Porridge)

As a child I remember looking forward to Moti Mummy's fasting days. She would sit apart from the rest of the family for her one meal of the day. We were not aware of the religious connotations of those days then. We just waited for her to be done so we would get to finish the leftovers. My personal favourite, was the morio (also called sama ni khichadi, sama ni khatti ghensh in Gujarati; and veru arisi in Tamil). The dish is cooked into a khichdi with sour buttermilk, potatoes and peanuts and spiked with the bite of green chillies. It retains its grainy texture on cooking and the potatoes absorb the sourness of the yoghurt and the spiciness of the chillies most deliciously.

Time: 30 minutes | Serves 2

Ingredients
- 200 gms sanwa millet (sama/morio)
- ½ tsp rock salt or to taste
- 2-3 green chillies, chopped
- 1" piece of fresh ginger, grated
- 1 tsp toasted cumin powder
- 1 cup sour buttermilk or sour yoghurt, whisked smooth
- 1 large potato, boiled, peeled and diced

Tempering
- 2 tbsp oil
- ½ tsp cumin seeds
- 2 dried red chillies
- 2 sprigs of curry leaves

Method

- Wash the millet thoroughly. Drain the water and set the damp millet aside for 30 minutes.
- Pour 2 cups of water into a wide kadhai or wok.
- Add the rock salt, green chillies, ginger and cumin powder and bring it to a boil on high heat.
- Put the oil for the tempering in a small pan on medium heat. When hot, add the cumin seeds and allow them to crackle. Add the red chillies and curry leaves.
- Mix this tempering into the seasoned and spiced water.
- Add the damp millet to the flavoured liquid and cook on medium heat for 10-12 minutes.
- Add the buttermilk or yoghurt along with the boiled potato. Mix thoroughly. At this point the consistency should be that of a loose runny porridge. If the water has dried out, add a little more and simmer for an additional 2 minutes.
- Remove from heat, cover and let it stand for 10 minutes.
- Serve hot.

Haldar Nu Athanu
(Fresh Turmeric Pickle)

This is an instant pickle my grandmother made when tender, fresh mango ginger came into season. Mango ginger, or amba haldi, is available during the monsoons. It has a strong aroma reminiscent of mango — that's the reason it is called amba haldi (amba means mango in many Indian languages). To it is added fresh root turmeric. It can be served with grilled dishes, paratha, khichdi, dal-chawal and virtually everything on the Indian menu. I also like it with my Thai meals.

Time: 20 minutes | Makes: 150 gms of pickle

Ingredients
- 100 gms fresh mango ginger (amba haldi), peeled and sliced or julienned
- 60 gms fresh turmeric root, peeled and sliced or julienned
- 3 green chillies, slit lengthwise but kept whole
- 4 tbsp lime juice
- 1 tsp salt

Method
- Combine all the ingredients in a bowl and mix well.
- This pickle is ready to serve after 1-2 hours.
- Store refrigerated in an airtight container or in a glass jar for up to 1 week.

Murrabba
(Mango Preserve)

Murabba, also called murabbo, along with the spicier chundo, were two staple preserves and pickles that were made every year by Moti Mummy. It was a favourite treat for us children; we ate it with hot, ghee-smeared rotis.

Time: 1 hour | Makes: 1 kg of preserve

Ingredients
- 250 gms raw green mangoes.
- 2 cups sugar.
- 2 x 1" cinnamon sticks.
- 2 cloves
- ½ tsp green cardamom seeds.
- A few saffron strands.

Method
- Wash the mangoes, peel them and grate coarsely.
- Heat ⅔ cup of water in a large pan and add the grated mangoes. Stir and cook uncovered for 4-5 minutes, till they soften.
- Strain and reserve the softened mangoes and the cooking liquid separately.
- Combine the sugar, mango liquid and an additional ½ cup of water in the same pan.
- Put the pan on medium heat and cook, stirring occasionally, till the sugar dissolves.
- Mix in the drained mangoes.
- Add the cinnamon and cloves and cook on low heat, till the syrup is of a 2-string consistency. (Place a little of the cooled syrup between your thumb and forefinger, and open them gently; two strings should be formed.)
- Remove from heat, add the cardamom seeds and saffron and mix well.
- Allow to cool completely and bottle in sterilised glass jars.

Leeli Mari Nu Athanu
(Green Peppercorn Pickle)

Green peppercorns are sold pickled in brine as a gourmet ingredient all over the world, a fact I discovered a few months after I became a food writer. I was much more familiar with them as the seasonal pickle that appeared at the dinner table every winter.

Green peppercorns are unripe pepper berries that would be dried into black and white pepper if their development were not arrested. I love green peppercorns for their bright, intense aroma, accented with hints of what I can only describe as 'green'. Their flavour is fresher than dried peppers and brings a piquant accent to dishes. The pickled ones work just as well as the fresh peppercorns. Use ground pickled peppercorns to flavour plain yoghurt in the summer, or stir it into cream sauces to go over pasta or chicken for festive dinners. A few bunches added whole to a Thai curry at the very end of cooking adds the pleasantly pungent surprise of them bursting between your teeth.

Time: 2 hours | Makes: 500 gms of pickle

Ingredients
- 150 gms pickling salt (salt that isn't iodised)
- 3½ tbsp lime juice, strained
- 100 gms fresh green peppercorn sprigs picked over, washed and air-dried
- 50 gms limes, quartered

Method
- Mix the salt with about 2 cups of water in a pan on high heat and bring to a boil. Continue to boil, till a rim of salt crystals forms on the sides of the pan.
- Skim and strain off any debris and cool.
- Stir in the lime juice.
- Add the peppercorns and limes, mix well and bottle.
- Close the bottle and keep it at room temperature in a cool, dark place. It will be

ready to eat in a week. It does not require refrigeration and will last for over a year. The peppercorn stalks will change to a somewhat dull, olive green colour; this is normal and doesn't change the quality of the pickle.

Note: This pickle tends to acquire a little mould on top where the peppercorns surface. Don't worry, simply pick out and discard the mouldy bits.

Mixed Vegetable Pickle

Crunchy vegetables pickled in brine and spiked with chilli and mustard made their appearance at the table every winter in this Indian version of piccalilli. I always wondered if it was indeed inspired by the piccalilli because, although it combines any fresh winter vegetables you like, it does comprise mainly 'English' vegetables such as cauliflower, carrot and green peas that are not traditional Gujarati preferences.

Time: 30 minutes + 24 hours for marination | Makes: 500 gms of pickle

Ingredients
- 250 gms mixed vegetables (carrot, cauliflower, green peas), diced
- 2 tbsp salt
- 2 tbsp split yellow mustard seeds
- 1½ tsp red chilli powder
- ¼ tsp asafoetida powder (hing)
- ½ tsp turmeric powder

Method
- Combine the mixed vegetables with salt and ½ cup of water and mix well. Transfer to a sterilised glass jar and leave for 1 day.
- The next day, strain out 2 tbsp of juices that have collected in the jar from the salted vegetables.
- To this, add the mustard seeds, chilli powder, asafoetida powder and turmeric powder and grind to a smooth paste in a blender.
- Add the resulting paste to the salted vegetables and mix well.
- Serve immediately or store refrigerated for up to 6 months.

Gujarati Kadhi
(Spicy Yoghurt Soup)

A Gujarati meal that we would have eaten in Moti Mummy's time.

Time: 20 minutes | Serves: 4

Ingredients
- 2 tbsp gram flour (besan)
- 1½ cups natural yoghurt, whisked smooth
- 1 tsp green chilli-ginger paste (see note on page 11)
- 2 curry leaves
- 2 tbsp sugar
- Salt to taste

Tempering
- 2 tsp ghee
- ½ tsp cumin seeds
- ½ tsp mustard seeds
- ½ tsp asafoetida powder (hing)
- 1 dried red chilli, broken into pieces

Garnish
- 2 tbsp chopped coriander leaves

Method
- Mix the gram flour with the yoghurt and 3 cups of water in a large pan and whisk, till well blended.
- Stir in the green chilli-ginger paste, curry leaves, sugar and salt.
- Put the pan on medium heat and bring to a boil, stirring all the while.
- Prepare the tempering by heating the ghee in a small pan and frying the cumin and mustard seeds, till they turn brown. Add the asafoetida powder and red chilli.
- Pour the tempering into the kadhi and boil for a few minutes.
- Sprinkle coriander leaves on top and serve hot.

Undhiyu
(Winter Vegetable Medley in Green Spices)

The vegetarian Gujarati community looks forward to the undhiyu season and gather for undhiyu parties just as other people come together for barbeques!

Traditional Indian dietetics believes that digestion is sluggish in certain seasons, and according to this seasonal eating pattern, winter means a celebration of the heavier spectrum of dishes of the Indian culinary repertoire.

However one chooses to eat undhiyu — with puri, steamed rice or just by itself as I do — it is essential to get one piece of each vegetable, even if it means you miss your next meal, because every bite should taste different, depending on the vegetable it contains. In fact, the sign of a good undhiyu is being unable to eat the next meal!

Time: 4 hours | Serves: 8-12

Ingredients

Muthia (spicy, fried gram flour and fenugreek leaf dumplings)

- 100 gms fenugreek leaves (methi)
- 1½ tbsp gram flour (besan)
- 2 garlic cloves, crushed
- 1 tsp carom seeds (ajwain)
- 2 tsp coriander-cumin powder
- 1 tsp red chilli powder
- 1 tsp turmeric powder
- 1 tsp sugar (optional)
- Salt to taste
- Oil as required

Green masala
- 3 cups coriander leaves
- 1 cup green spring garlic, finely chopped
- 1 fresh coconut, grated
- 1 tsp salt or to taste

Vegetables
- 250 gms Surti papdi (see notes)
- 250 gms fresh green pigeon peas (toover/arhar)
- 200 gms tender green peas, in their shells
- 250 gms small potatoes, kept whole
- 200 gms purple yam (kand)
- 200 gms elephant yam (suran)
- 200 gms sweet potatoes
- 200 gms aubergines (baingan)
- 4 semi-ripe, yellow Rajagiri bananas, left unpeeled
- 50 gms Surti ariya kakdi (see notes)

Tempering
- 1 cup oil
- 1½ tsp carom seeds (ajwain)
- ½ tsp asafoetida powder (hing)

Garnish
- 2 tbsp coarsely chopped tender green garlic shoots

Method

Muthia
- Pluck out the fenugreek leaves and discard the stems and roots. Wash the leaves thoroughly in several changes of water. Drain well and place them in a bowl.
- Add the remaining ingredients and mix well.
- Shape the mixture into walnut-sized round dumplings adding water and oil as required.
- Steam the muthia for 15-20 minutes, till soft and firm.
- Put the oil for shallow-frying in a pan on medium heat. When hot, lightly fry

the muthia, till crisp on the outside.
- Set aside to drain on kitchen paper.

Green masala
- Wash the coriander leaves thoroughly in several changes of water. Drain well and chop coarsely.
- Grind all the ingredients to make a coarse paste.

Vegetables
- Top, tail and string the papdi. Split them and cut into half.
- Shell the green lentils and green peas.
- Keep the potatoes unpeeled and whole. Scrub them thoroughly.
- Cut off the aubergine crowns and slit them cross-wise.
- Peel both the yams, wash thoroughly and cut into large square chunks.
- Keep the sweet potatoes unpeeled, wash thoroughly and cut into large chunks.
- Keep the bananas unpeeled and cut into chunks.
- Cut the kakdi into chunks.
- Stuff or mix the vegetables, keeping each one separate, with half the green masala.

Undhiyu
- Heat the oil for the tempering in a large pan that has a tight-fitting lid, in which you will cook the undhiyu. Sauté the carom seeds and asafoetida powder for a few seconds.
- Spread the vegetables in the pan in layers. Lay the foundation with the Surti papdi, green lentils and green peas.
- Then layer the vegetables in progression of cooking time starting with the potatoes followed by the aubergines, both the yams, sweet potatoes and bananas. Add the muthiya.
- Top with the Surti ariya kakdi.
- Smother everything with the remaining aromatic green masala.
- Cover the pan and leave the undhiyu to simmer slowly over very low heat in its own juices, untouched for 1½-2 hours, till the vegetables are cooked to tenderness.
- To serve, invert the entire assembly on to a serving platter and top with the chopped garlic shoots.

Notes:
- *Surti papdi is a flat, jade-green, delicate field bean only found in Surat in the winter and is an essential ingredient in undhiyu.*
- *Ariya kakdi is a tough-skinned zucchini-like seedless cucumber, omit if you cannot get it.*

Khamang Kakdi
(Coconut Cucumber Salad)

This is a refreshing traditional Gujarati salad.

Time: 10 minutes | Serves: 4

Ingredients
- 2 tsp oil
- 1 tsp sesame seeds (til)
- 1 tsp cumin seeds
- ½ cup peanuts, roasted and coarsely crushed
- 1 tsp rock salt
- 200 gms cucumbers, peeled and diced
- 2 tbsp chopped coriander leaves
- ½ tbsp lime juice
- ½ tsp sugar

Method
- Heat the oil in a kadhai or wok and add the sesame seeds and cumin seeds. When they crackle, add the peanuts and salt and sauté on medium heat for a minute.
- Remove from heat.
- Add the cucumbers and coriander leaves and mix well.
- Just before serving mix in the lime juice and sugar.
- Serve immediately.

Methi Thepla
(Fenugreek-flavoured Flatbread)

Time: 30 minutes | Makes: 12-14 flatbreads

Ingredients
- ½ cup fenugreek leaves (methi)
- 2 cups wholewheat flour (atta) + extra for rolling
- 1 cup yoghurt, whisked smooth
- ½ tsp turmeric powder
- 1½ tsp red chilli powder
- 1 tbsp coriander powder
- 2 tbsp oil + extra for smearing
- Salt to taste

Method
- Pluck out the fenugreek leaves and discard the stems and roots. Wash the leaves thoroughly in several changes of water. Drain well and chop fine.
- Mix all the ingredients together in a bowl and knead into a soft, smooth dough using water only if required.
- Divide the dough into 12-14 equal portions and shape into balls.
- Roll each portion on a lightly floured surface into a 5" round thepla; they should be translucent.
- Put a tava or griddle on medium heat. When hot, put a thepla on the tava and smear a little oil on both sides. Cook, till brown spots appear on the base. Turn over and cook the other side.
- Serve hot.

Variation: *Doodhi Thepla – Add ¾ cup of grated white pumpkin instead of the fenugreek leaves while making the dough and proceed as given. Adjust the seasoning to taste.*

Chak Chak

There is a set of soup plates at my Nani's house that I covet. On the face of it, there's nothing exceptional about them. They are simple bone china plates adorned with a pink floral design. Of the odd number left, some are chipped and others are covered in a webbing of cracks; but I covet them. I covet them real bad! To me they are symbolic of the unique person that is my grandmother.

The entire dinner service was bought as a result of my Nani's successful orchestration of a full Continental meal. Tomato soup, baked beans and macaroni might not appear like such a big deal today, but imagine cooking up a spread like this decades ago — entirely based on imagination after just a taste. But I am getting ahead of myself.

I had sensed early on that there was something special about my maternal lineage. Even as a child I noted that people from that side of the family made it a point to describe themselves as Kutchi Bhatia when introduced as Gujarati.

Kutchi food is often lost under the larger classification of Gujarati food, but is actually distinct in its own right. Although there are some traditional meals unique to the Kutchi Bhatias, there are several dishes common to both. But the difference is noticeable in the style of preparation; Gujarati food tends to be oily and leans towards sweet, heavily-spiced fried foods, whereas Kutchi Bhatia food is based on fresh seasonal ingredients cooked in minimal oil and leelo masallo (a fresh green spice paste of ground ginger and green chillies). Spicing is used to complement the dish being cooked, at no point overwhelming the natural flavour of the food. Gud or sugar are selectively used in dishes where a balance of flavours needs to be achieved.

With so much importance given to seasonal foods and minimal spicing, it is no surprise that eating out was frowned upon. Wherever Nani's family went, food would be catered from home kitchens, overseen by her and sent along. When the family moved to Lonavala in the summer months, the entire household moved. In fact, even if the family went to catch a play at the local theatre, Poria (the faithful manservant) would be waiting outside in time for the interval, tiffin basket in hand.

So when my grandfather started frequenting clubs — a legacy of the Raj — and encouraged Nani to try things and figure out how they were made, Nani took up the challenge to cook an 'English meal'. Over time, her Continental meals became legendary and when they were on the menu, her brothers-in-law would get excited and say 'aaje ghar ma chak chak thasé' today there will be chak chak in the house. (Chak chak was the sound made by salt and pepper shakers which were associated with English or Continental food.)

This sense of culinary adventure is her legacy to me. Today, when I taste a dish and figure out what has gone into it and then recreate it from memory, I have her to thank.

Nani's Milk Bread

Time: 1 hour + overnight for fermentation + 2-3 hours for the dough to rise | Makes: 2 loaves or 12-16 buns

Ingredients
- 1 litre milk
- ½ cup husked, split Bengal gram (chana dal)
- 500 gms refined flour (maida)
- 1 tsp sodium bicarbonate
- Ghee for greasing

Method
- Bring the milk to a boil on high heat.
- Put the dal in a bowl and pour the hot milk over it. Cover and leave to ferment overnight.
- Rub the mixture through a sieve and strain into a bowl. Discard the dal.
- Sift the flour and sodium bicarbonate three times into a bowl.
- Add the flour to the milk and mix to make a batter of dropping consistency.
- Grease 2 small loaf tins or 12-16 katoris with ghee and spoon in the batter to come one-third of the way up.
- Place in a warm place, till the dough rises to the top of the tins or katoris.
- Bake in an oven preheated to 180°C for about 1 hour, till the tops are a light golden.
- Test by inserting a skewer into the centre of the bread; if it comes out clean, it is ready, else bake for another 5 minutes and test again.
- Allow to cool slightly and turn out on to a wire rack to cool completely.
- The base will be nicely browned.

Nani's Date Cake

Time: 1 hour 20 minutes | Makes: 1 cake

Ingredients
- 2½ cups refined flour (maida)
- 100 gms butter
- 1 tbsp baking powder
- 1 tbsp sodium bicarbonate
- ½ cup milk
- 1 tsp vanilla extract
- 1 kg seedless dates, chopped
- 1 cup sugar, powdered
- 2 tbsp walnuts, chopped

Method
- Sift the flour three times into a bowl.
- Add the butter and rub it in, till it resembles breadcrumbs.
- Combine the baking powder, sodium bicarbonate, milk and vanilla extract in a small bowl and mix, till well blended.
- Add it to the flour. Mix well again.
- Fold in the dates, sugar and walnuts.
- Spoon the batter into a greased 12" round cake tin.
- Bake the cake in an oven preheated to 180°C for 45 minute to 1 hour, till it rises well and is cooked.
- Test by inserting a skewer into the centre of the cake; if it comes out clean, it is ready, else bake for another 5 minutes and test again.
- Turn out on to a wire rack and allow to cool completely.

Copra Pak
(Coconut Fudge)

Time: 35 minutes | Makes: 20 pieces

Ingredients
- 1 tsp warm milk
- A few saffron strands
- 2 cups sugar
- 1 tsp lime juice
- 2 cups grated fresh coconut
- 2 tsp ghee1/3 tsp green cardamom powder

Method
- Put the warm milk in a small bowl, add the saffron and rub it in, till dissolved. Reserve.
- Dissolve the sugar in 1 cup of water in a pan on medium heat and bring it to a boil.
- Add the lime juice to clarify the syrup. (It binds with impurities and brings them to the surface.) Skim off the resultant scummy debris that floats to the top.
- Alternatively, strain the syrup though a strainer lined with muslin cloth.
- Bring the syrup to a boil again and cook, till it is of a 2-string consistency. (Place a little of the cooled syrup between your thumb and forefinger, and open them gently; two strings should be formed.)
- Stir in the coconut, ghee, cardamom powder and dissolved saffron.
- Remove from heat stirring continuously.
- Carefully spread the mixture on a lightly greased thali or rimmed plate, till cool.
- Cut into diamond shapes and serve or store in a clean, dry airtight container.

Khara Ané Mitha Chavda Or Pudla
(Sweet and Spicy Crêpes)

A classic meal of the Kutchi Bhatia community is that of the khara and mitha chavda — wheat crêpes — some of which are savoury and the rest sweetened with jaggery.

Time: 20 minutes + 1 hour for batter to rest | Serves: 4-6

Ingredients
Sweet crêpes

- 1 cup wholewheat flour (atta)
- ¼ cup powdered sugar or grated jaggery
- ½ cup ghee or oil for shallow-frying

To serve the sweet crêpes

- 4 tbsp powdered sugar

Savoury crêpes

- ¼ tsp turmeric powder
- 1 tsp coriander powder
- 1 tsp cumin powder
- 1 tsp green chilli-ginger paste (see note on page 11)
- 1 small onion, finely chopped
- 1 small tomato, finely chopped (optional)
- Salt to taste
- 2 cups gram flour (besan)
- ½ cup ghee or oil for shallow-frying

Method
Sweet crêpes

- Combine the flour, sugar and ¾ cup of water in a large mixing bowl of about 1 kg capacity.

- Mix to make a semi-liquid batter ensuring that there are no lumps. Cover and set aside for 1 hour.
- Put a tava or griddle on medium heat. When hot, spread a little ghee or oil over it.
- Pour a large spoonful of the batter on the tava or griddle, spreading it with the back of the spoon to form a thin round crêpe.
- Spread some ghee or oil over the surface of the crêpe and around its edges. Carefully turn over once or twice, till done.
- Remove when crisp and sprinkle with powdered sugar.
- Make all the crêpes in the same way.

Savoury crêpes

- Combine the spice powders, green chilli-ginger paste, onion and tomato (if using) in a large mixing bowl of about 1 kg capacity.
- Mix the gram flour and slowly pour in up to 1 cup of water, stirring continuously to avoid lumps. Whisk well to make a semi-liquid batter.
- Add salt to taste.
- Cook the crêpes as given for the sweet ones.

Sama Sabudana Dhokla
(Sanwa Millet and Sago Cakes)

Time: 1 hour + 4 hours for batter to rest | Serves: 2-4

Ingredients
- 250 gms sanwa millet (sama)
- 100 gms pearl sago (sabudana)
- 2 cups sour buttermilk
- Rock salt to taste
- ½ tsp green chilli-ginger paste (see note on page 11)
- 1 tsp oil
- ½ tsp sodium bicarbonate
- Ghee for greasing

Tempering
- 2 tbsp ghee
- ½ tsp cumin seeds

Garnish
- ½ cup grated fresh coconut
- 1 tbsp finely chopped coriander leaves

Method
- Grind the millet and sago in a dry grinder to make a grainy flour.
- Transfer to a bowl and add the buttermilk gradually, stirring continuously, till it reaches the consistency of a thick batter. Cover and leave to rest for 4 hours.
- Add salt to taste, green chilli-ginger paste, oil and sodium bicarbonate. Mix well.
- Grease two thalis or rimmed plates well with ghee and pour the batter to come halfway up the sides.
- Tap the sides to even out the surface.
- Steam over hot water for 10 minutes.
- Remove and when cool, cut into squares.

- Put the ghee for the tempering in a small pan on medium heat. When hot, add the cumin seeds. Allow to crackle and pour the tempering over the dhoklas.
- Garnish with coconut and coriander leaves and serve.

Pattice
(Coriander-stuffed Potato Fritters)

Time: 1 hour | Makes: 12-18 patties

Ingredients
- 500 gms potatoes
- 2 tbsp arrowroot flour
- Rock salt to taste

Filling
- 50 gms coriander leaves
- 100 gms fresh coconut, grated
- ½ tsp cumin powder
- 2 tsp lime juice
- 1 tsp green chilli-ginger-paste (see note on page 11)
- 1 tsp rock salt

To assemble and fry the fritters
- 1 tbsp arrowroot flour + extra for dusting
- 300 ml peanut oil

Method
- Wash the potatoes and boil them, till tender.
- When cool enough to handle, peel and mash them in a bowl.
- Add 1 tbsp of arrowroot flour and salt to taste. Mix well and set aside.

Filling
- Wash the coriander leaves thoroughly in several changes of water. Drain well and chop fine.
- Combine all the filling ingredients in another bowl and mix well.

To assemble the fritters
- Divide the mashed potato into 12-18 portions.

- Dust your hands with some arrowroot flour and make a thin disc with one portion.
- Place ½ tsp of filling in the centre and bring the potato disc together around the filling to make a ball. Repeat with the remaining portions.
- Put the oil in a kadhai or wok on medium heat. When hot, roll the balls in arrowroot flour and fry them in batches, till golden. Take care not to stir too much as they could burst.

Note: Nani does an interesting faraali or fasting version of this pattice, using purple yam or kand instead of the potatoes.

Tapkhir Khandvi
(Spiced Buttermilk Squares or Rolls)

This recipe is a classic example of my Nani's creativity. Her variation of the traditional khandvi uses arrowroot flour and rock salt, making it appropriate to eat on fasting days.

Time: 1 hour | Serves: 2

Ingredients
- 250 gms arrowroot flour
- 1 tsp rock salt
- 1 tsp green chilli-ginger paste (see note on page 11)
- 1 cup sour buttermilk
- 1 tbsp oil for greasing

Tempering
- 1 tbsp oil
- ½ tsp cumin seeds

Garnish
- 2 tbsp grated fresh coconut
- 2 tbsp chopped coriander leaves

Method
- Place the arrowroot flour in a large mixing bowl of about 1 kg capacity.
- Add salt, green chilli-ginger paste, buttermilk and 1 cup of water, stirring well to break up any lumps that form.
- Pour the mixture into a medium-sized non-stick kadhai or wok and cook on medium heat, stirring all the while, till the mixture thickens and begins to leave the sides of the pan.
- Grease a thali or rimmed plate with oil and pour the mixture into it, spreading evenly into a very thin layer.
- Allow it to cool and cut into diamond shapes.

- Alternatively, cut it into strips and roll them like the traditional khandvi.
- Arrange the khandvi on a flat serving platter.
- Put the oil for the tempering in a small pan on medium heat. When hot, add the cumin seeds. When they crackle, pour the tempering over the khandvi.
- Garnish with coconut and coriander leaves and serve.

Chundo
(Spicy Mango Pickle)

Chundo is a grated mango pickle that is sweet and hot. When made right it has the consistency of marmalade but with lots of grated slivers of mango in it. It spreads easily on to anything and can be used as a relish. The simple ingredients also make it ideal in the hotter summer months.

Time: 1 hour + 8-21 days to sun the pickle | Makes: 1½ kg of pickle

Ingredients
- 3 raw, firm Rajapuri mangoes
- Sugar, 1½ times the volume of the mango
- ½ cup salt
- 1 tbsp turmeric powder
- 2 tbsp red chilli powder
- 1 tbsp cumin seeds, crushed coarsely

Method
- Wash the mangoes and dry thoroughly. Peel and grate them. Measure out the quantity of mango in cups.
- Measure out 1½ times the same volume of sugar and set aside.
- Mix the mangoes with the salt and turmeric powder and set aside for about 30 minutes.
- Take handfuls of the grated mango and squeeze gently to remove excess water. Transfer the squeezed mango to a clean stainless steel thali or tray.
- Add the measured sugar and mix well.
- Tie a piece of muslin cloth over the thali or tray and place in the sun.
- If you want to do it right and have the patience, then, like my Nani, leave your chundo in the sun for 8-21 days. This means that it goes out every morning (after a stir) and comes in every night. You will know your pickle is done when the sugar has melted to a syrup and has a 1½-2-string consistency. (Place a

little of the cooled syrup between your thumb and forefinger and open them gently; 1½-2 strings should be formed.)
- Stir in the chilli powder and crushed cumin seeds.
- Take care not to touch a wet spoon to the pickle. There is an easier option, but be warned it will not taste the same. It is almost as though the flavour of sunlight is captured in this pickle! Place a heavy-bottomed pan on low heat and put the mango-sugar mixture in it. Cook, till all the water has evaporated, stirring to avoid sticking, till it reaches the correct consistency.
- Add the chilli powder and crushed cumin seeds while still hot.

Notes: There are a few variables you need to watch out for with chundo:
- *Mangoes: In case the mangoes are not firm, i.e. have begun to ripen, they will not do for chundo. The recipe calls for Rajapuri mangoes; these are large and used raw, sour and firm. The idea being that the pickle, when ready, should hold the form of the slivers it has been grated into.*
- *The sun: The sun may not be strong where you live, so vary the number of days you sun the chundo accordingly. If it's really hot, then 3-4 days will suffice, but if the intensity is lower, the number of days will vary between 4-8 days. It can go up to 21 days. Just keep an eye on it.*
- *Crystallisation: If you notice that there the sugar is crystallising, then the sugar ratio is too high. Grate some more mango, salt it, squeeze, mix it in.*
- *Ants: Chundo is an ant magnet! The muslin cloth is to keep them and other stuff that might get in, out. If ants are a problem where you live, take the extra precaution of placing the whole container of chundo in a basin of water. Don't let water get into the pickle however.*
- *Variation: This is something I like to do with a small batch: increase the chilli quotient and add raisins when I add the chilli powder.*

Methambo
(Mango Pickle)

Yes, I have got one more recipe with green mango, to fill in the gap while the sun cooks your pickle. It also uses up the little bits closer to the stone that can't be grated. It is a sort of consolation for those who have a riper mango and can't do the chundo. The addition of the spices and use of jaggery make methambo ideal in colder climates.

Time: 2 hours | Makes: 1½-2 kg of pickle

Ingredients
- 1 kg raw green mangoes
- 3 tbsp salt
- 2 tbsp turmeric powder
- 2 tbsp oil
- 1 tsp mustard seeds
- 8-10 dried red, round boria chillies
- 2 tbsp coriander seeds
- 7-8 cloves
- 7-8 x 1" cinnamon sticks
- 60 gms seedless raisins
- 1 kg jaggery, finely sliced
- 2 tbsp red chilli powder

Method
- Wash the mangoes and dry completely. Peel and chop the flesh fine.
- Put the chopped mangoes in a large mixing bowl.
- Mix in the salt and turmeric powder, and set aside for an hour or so, till the juices of the fruit are released.
- Strain the mangoes through a strainer or colander, but do not press.
- Put the oil in a large pan on medium heat. When hot, add the mustard seeds

and red chillies. When the seeds crackle, add the coriander seeds, cloves and cinnamon sticks.
- Wait for 2 seconds to allow the aromas to develop.
- Reduce the heat to low and add the mangoes, raisins and jaggery, stirring all the while. Cook, till uniformly thick.
- Add the chilli powder just before you take it off the heat.
- On cooling the methambo will thicken further.
- Store in a clean, dry, airtight jar.

Tapkhir Jo Halvo
(Arrowroot Fudge)

Tapkhir is arrowroot flour. A starch extract of the root of a tropical plant native to the Americas called maranta, it is used for its thickening characteristics. When heated the starch turns to jelly and so thickens the liquid. It offers the added advantage of being completely tasteless compared to other flours. It also cooks to a clear finish. It is a favourite thickening agent in the Kutchi kitchen. Nani loved to experiment with it.

Time: 35 minutes | Makes: 20 pieces

Ingredients
- 1 cup arrowroot flour
- 1¼ cups sugar
- 2 tsp ghee
- 4-5 almonds, finely sliced
- A few green cardamom seeds
- A few saffron strands

Method
- Mix 1½ cups of water with the arrowroot flour in a bowl and set aside.
- Put the sugar in a pan with 1½ cups of water and bring to a boil on high heat. When the sugar has dissolved completely, add the arrowroot-water mix and stir well.
- When the mix starts to thicken, add the ghee and almonds and stir well. Let it thicken some more, till it starts to leave the sides of the pan.
- Add the cardamom and saffron and stir well.
- Pour the mix into a lightly greased thali or rimmed plate, till cool and set.
- Cut into diamond shapes and serve or store in a clean, dry, airtight container.

Lachko or Kathan Dal
(Thick, Tempered Lentils)

Time: 20 minutes | Serves: 4-6

Ingredients
- 1 cup husked, split pigeon peas (toover/arhar dal)
- 1" piece of fresh ginger, finely sliced
- ¼ tsp turmeric powder
- Salt to taste

Tempering
- 1 tbsp ghee
- ¼ tsp asafoetida powder (hing)

Method
- Wash the dal and pressure-cook it with the ginger, turmeric powder and 4-5 cups of water for 5-7 minutes on low heat, after the cooker reaches full pressure.
- Remove from heat and set aside, till the pressure subsides.
- Open the cooker and drain out the water from the top of the dal into a bowl. Use it for kadhi or osaman.
- Transfer the dal to a pan.
- Put the ghee for the tempering in a small pan on medium heat. When hot, add the asafoetida powder.
- Pour the contents of the pan over the cooked dal.
- Churn the dal to a smooth consistency.
- Return to heat, add salt to taste and let it simmer for about 10 minutes.
- When it is thick, remove from heat and serve with rice and kadhi (page 19) or osaman (page 46).

Osaman
(Spicy Thin Lentil Soup)

A Kutchi meal from my Nani's table.

Time: 40 minutes | Serves: 6

Ingredients

- ½ cup husked, split pigeon peas (toover/arhar dal)
- 1 tsp green chilli-ginger paste (see note on page 11)
- 4-6 pieces of kokum
- 2 tbsp grated jaggery or to taste
- ½ tsp turmeric powder
- Salt to taste

Tempering

- 1 tbsp ghee
- ¼ tsp fenugreek seeds (methi)
- ¼ tsp mustard seeds
- ¼ tsp cumin seeds
- ¼ tsp asafoetida powder (hing)
- A few curry leaves
- 1 green chilli, slit
- 2" piece of white radish, finely sliced

Garnish

- 2 tbsp grated fresh coconut
- 2 tbsp chopped coriander leaves

Method

- Wash the dal and pressure-cook it with 4 cups of water for 5-7 minutes on low heat, after the cooker reaches full pressure.
- Remove from heat and set aside, till the pressure subsides.
- Open the cooker and churn the dal well.

- Transfer to a pan.
- Add the green chilli-ginger paste, kokum, jaggery, turmeric powder and salt to taste.
- Put the pan on high heat and boil the dal for 10-15 minutes.
- Put the ghee for the tempering in a small pan on medium heat. When hot, add the fenugreek seeds, mustard seeds and cumin seeds. When they crackle, add the asafoetida powder, curry leaves, green chilli and radish.
- Pour the tempering over the osaman. Simmer for 10 minutes.
- Garnish with coconut and coriander leaves.
- Serve hot with kathan dal (page 45) and steamed white rice.

Sambhariye Jo Shaak
(Stuffed Mixed Vegetables)

Time: 1 hour | Serves: 6-8

Ingredients

Vegetables

- 400 gms small potatoes, peeled
- 300 gms small onions, peeled
- 300 gms small aubergines (baingan)

Filling

- ½ cup finely chopped coriander leaves
- 1 cup gram flour (besan)
- 2 tbsp oil
- ¾ cup grated fresh coconut
- 1 tbsp coriander powder
- 1 tbsp cumin powder
- 1 tbsp green chilli-ginger paste (see note on page 11)
- 2 tsp sugar
- 1 tsp red chilli powder
- Juice of 1 lime
- Salt to taste

Tempering

- 6 tbsp oil
- ½ tsp mustard seeds
- ¼ tsp fenugreek seeds (methi)
- 3-4 green chillies, slit
- ¼ tsp asafoetida powder (hing)
- A few curry leaves

Method

- Make a slit in the potatoes and onions vertically, without separating the pieces and immerse them in water.
- Remove the stem from the aubergines and make a vertical slit without separating the pieces.
- Wash the coriander leaves thoroughly in several changes of water. Drain well and chop fine. Reserve.
- Roast the gram flour on a tava or griddle on low heat, till fragrant. Transfer to a bowl and mix in the oil.
- Add the remaining filling ingredients and mix well.
- Stuff the masala filling into the slits of all the vegetables. If there is extra, set it aside to sprinkle on top.
- Put the oil for the tempering in a large, wide pan on medium heat. When hot, add the mustard seeds, fenugreek seeds and green chillies.
- When they crackle, add the asafoetida powder and curry leaves.
- Place all the vegetables in turn very gently in the pan. Cover with a rimmed plate, and put water in it. This will help the vegetables to cook on medium heat, and prevent the them from sticking.
- When half-cooked, after about 20 minutes or so, remove the lid. Sprinkle any remaining masala filling.
- Stir gently and continue cooking on medium heat, till the vegetables are tender.
- Remove from heat and cover.
- Turn the vegetables out onto a deep serving platter and serve hot with rotis.

Khatta Dhokla
(Spicy Sour Buttermilk Steamed Cakes)

Time: 30-40 minutes + overnight for soaking + 5-6 hours for fermentation | Serves: 4-6

Ingredients
- 3 cups rice
- 1 cup whole black gram (sabut urad)
- 1 cup sour yoghurt, whisked smooth
- 6 green chillies
- 1" piece of fresh ginger, chopped
- ¾ tsp sodium bicarbonate
- 3 tbsp oil
- ¼ tsp asafoetida powder (hing)
- Salt to taste

Garnish
- Black pepper powder or red chilli powder

Method
- Mix the rice and dal and grind it coarsely, till it has the consistency of semolina.
- Alternatively, soak the rice and dal in plenty of water overnight. Drain thoroughly and grind them the next morning.
- Transfer to a bowl and add the yoghurt and just enough hot water to make a thick paste.
- Cover and leave to ferment for 5-6 hours so that the mixture becomes slightly sour.
- Grind the green chillies and ginger to make a paste and add it to the batter, along with the sodium bicarbonate, oil, asafoetida powder and salt to taste. Mix well.
- Grease 2 thalis or rimmed plates, small enough to fit into your pressure cooker.

- Fill them with batter to come one-third of the way up.
- Dust with pepper or chilli powder.
- Steam for 10 minutes in a pressure-cooker without the pressure weight.
- Alternatively, use an idli steamer.
- Cut into diamond shapes and serve.

Nani's Special Chaas
(Buttermilk)

Chaas is nothing but deliciously spiced buttermilk. It is ideal for a hot summer afternoon as a coolant or to appease your palate after a heavy or spicy meal. Chaas makes a delicious accompaniment to Handvo (page 10). This thin cool buttermilk is intrinsic to the Kutchi meal and is called 'Kutchi beer' because it was served in beer bottles.

Time: 5 minutes | Serves: 4

Ingredients

- 200 ml fresh yoghurt, whisked smooth
- 1 tsp cumin powder
- 5-6 mint leaves, roughly torn
- Salt to taste

Method

- Combine all the ingredients in a tall jug and pour in 400 ml of chilled water. Use a hand blender or whisk to blend the buttermilk to a smooth, thin consistency.
- Chill, till ready to drink.
- The solids will settle to the bottom, but don't worry, just give it a stir before serving.

Spice of Life

It really doesn't matter how old you are, if you marry, become a mother yourself, twice, set up your own business and (hopefully) go on to conquer the world — your mother is always the source of infinite patience and calm. A bowl of her patented dal soup still has the power to fill the holes caused by any pain or fright that life brings and her arms offer shelter from everything.

Putting all that is my mother into mere words will not do justice to her, in fact it seems a temerity. But if I am to tell the story of my culinary coming-of-age, it would be incomplete without her influence. Of all the women in my life, my mother has been the strongest influence on my cooking.

My mother, Heena Munshaw is an incredible woman. She survived the loss of her husband and steered her family through the ups and downs of financial and emotional hardships with amazing grace and strength. She is also an exceptional cook and carries forward the culinary traditions of her own and her husband's side of the family.

But none of this was evident in the Heena who got married at eighteen. She could not cook anything then. In fact, the first thing she ever cooked in her life was baked potato croquettes with a tomato sauce for her dad and her fiancé to be (my father). And as a young married woman whenever she was given a kitchen task in her new home, she would call her mother, and Poria, the faithful retainer in her maternal home, would arrive at her in-laws' under some pretext and perform her share of the task. I am always surprised by this story of my mother's early life, because the mother I know could not cook badly if her life depended on it! The most memorable dishes she cooked were her renditions of Indian Chinese. My parents ate out a lot, and Mom, ever her mother's daughter, having eaten at China Garden often, managed to recreate an entire Chinese meal at home, some picked up from culinary legend, Nelson Wang, whose restaurant China Garden was the hottest place to go to, and many, using her own creativity.

The singular quality I am proud to have inherited from my mother, is her ability to reinvent herself into the cook that the person she is cooking for needs her to be. For instance, taking the trouble to cook an egg-free soup for my grandmother so she could enjoy that Indian Chinese meal as well; or, mindful of my juvenile diabetic cousin, braise garlic in oil and stir-fry vegetables for him, instead of feeding him the unhealthy vegetable sweet-sour full of sugar and cornflour.

Like mother, like daughter. Food has become an extension of love for me, and through it I have learned to go the extra mile for those I love, so that they feel treasured in my life.

Dudhi Nu Shaak
(Bottle Gourd Stew)

My mother laughed when I asked her for this recipe; she couldn't believe I wanted to put it in the book. But too often we dwell on the fancy and complicated recipes, forgetting that there is great flavour in the simple ones of everyday cooking.

The trick to this recipe is to cook the gourd just right. I call it al dente, when the gourd chunks are cooked through but still offer firmness to the teeth.

Time: 30 minutes | Serves: 2-4

Ingredients
- 1½ tbsp oil
- ½ tsp cumin seeds
- 1-2 green chillies, sliced lengthwise in half
- A few fresh curry leaves
- 500 gms bottle gourd (lauki/ghia/doodhi)5-6 medium-sized tomatoes, cubed

Method
- Peel the gourd and cut the flesh into large chunks, discarding the seeds.
- Put the oil in a non-stick pan on medium heat. When hot, add the cumin seeds. Allow them to crackle and then add the green chillies and curry leaves.
- Wait for 10 seconds for the curry leaves to crackle and then add the gourd and sufficient water to cover it. Allow it to boil, till almost cooked but al dente or firm to the teeth.
- Add the tomatoes and simmer, till they are soft but be careful and time it right so the gourd is not overcooked. Serve hot.

Spice Of Life

This is the legendary chutney that inspired the title of this chapter. My mother's patent chutney was christened 'spice of life' by us, her kids, because this hot, sweet, spicy, sour, absolutely delicious condiment has travelled with us through our lives, enlivening insipid hostel food and spicing up bland food on our travels. Later in life, it saved many a day when amateur attempts at cooking went wrong and it soon became the secret ingredient in a myriad of dishes from dum aloo to Schezwan chicken, and spicy jacket potatoes. I can never make it quite like she does, but I still try ever so often.

It is advisable to use a heavy-bottomed pan so that the ingredients do not stick.

Time: 2 hours + overnight for soaking | Makes: 1 kg of chutney

Ingredients

- 500 gms dried red Kashmiri chillies
- 300 gms garlic, peeled
- 2 cups white vinegar
- 1 kg tomato purée
- 1 cup oil
- 4-5 cloves
- 4-5 whole black peppercorns
- 2 x 1" cinnamon sticks
- 3½ cups sugar
- 2 tbsp red Kashmiri chilli powder or to taste

Method

- Soak the red chillies and the garlic in vinegar overnight. This will ensure that the garlic does not spoil.

- The next day, grind the soaked chilli-garlic mixture in a blender to a coarse purée. If you need to add lubrication, use the tomato purée, do not use water. Avoid the use of water completely.
- Put the oil in a heavy-bottomed pan on medium heat. When hot, add the whole spices, the chilli-garlic paste, tomato purée and sugar. Simmer, till the oil separates.
- Stir in the chilli powder and simmer for another minute.
- Remove, cool and bottle. This lasts more than a year at room temperature. (If it is allowed to, that is!)

Dal Soup
(Tempered Lentil Soup)

A bowl of my mother's patented dal soup was always the perfect antidote for whatever ailed me. For years now, I have been cooking this soup, but have never quite achieved the same intensity of curry flavour that my mother's version has. I always thought it was that 'haath ka kamaal' (the belief that every cook brings their own special touch to a recipe, and while others may follow the same recipe accurately, it will still taste best made by that one person's hand), but that wasn't it. I found out while I was going over the recipe for this book that an essential ingredient had been missed — the curry powder in the tempering!

Time: 25 minutes | Serves: 4 as a soup, 3 as an entrée

Ingredients
- 1 cup husked, split Egyptian lentils (masoor dal)
- 3-4 medium-sized onions, quartered
- 6 large tomatoes, blanched, peeled and quartered
- 5-6 garlic cloves, halved
- 1" piece of fresh ginger, coarsely chopped
- ½ tsp red chilli powder (optional)
- Salt to taste
- 1 litre water or vegetable stock

Tempering
- 1 tbsp ghee
- 2 bay leaves
- ½" cinnamon stick
- 3-4 cloves
- ½ tsp curry powder (commercial)

Method

- Wash the dal thoroughly under cold running water.
- Combine the dal, onions, tomatoes, garlic, ginger, chilli powder (if using), salt and water or stock in a pressure cooker and pressure-cook for 3-4 minutes on low heat, after the cooker reaches full pressure.
- Alternatively, cook in a pan on medium heat for 7-10 minutes, till the dal is tender.
- Remove from heat and let it cool a little.
- Process the dal in a blender and strain into a large pan.
- Temper just before you serve. If the soup has cooled down please reheat and bring to a boil before you start the tempering.
- Put the ghee in a small pan on medium heat. When hot, add the whole spices and stir, till the aromas are released.
- Add the curry powder and give it a quick stir.
- Quickly pour the tempering over the boiling soup. Stir and cover.
- Uncover at the table, else the aroma will quickly fade away.

Serving suggestions: *Serve as a soup with chopped onions, lime wedges and buttered fresh pao on the side. Serve accompanied by steamed white rice and a salad of finely chopped onion, tomato and cucumber. This makes a quick, wholesome and supremely satisfying meal.*

Khatta Moong
(Spicy Whole Moong Bean and Yoghurt Soup)

Time: 40 minutes | Serves: 4

Ingredients
- 1 cup whole green moong beans
- 1 cup sour yoghurt, whisked smooth
- ½ tsp green chilli-ginger paste (see note on page 11)
- 2 tbsp oil
- 1 tsp mustard seeds
- ¼ tsp asafoetida powder (hing) or 3½ garlic cloves, crushed
- 3-4 curry leaves
- 1 green chilli, chopped
- ½ tsp turmeric powder
- Salt to taste

Garnish
- 2 tbsp finely chopped coriander leaves

Method
- Wash the beans and pressure-cook them with 3 cups of water for 5-7 minutes on low heat, after the cooker reaches full pressure.
- Remove from heat and set aside, till the pressure subsides.
- The beans should be tender and falling apart. Strain and reserve the beans and cooking water.
- Beat the sour yoghurt with 1 cup of the reserved cooking water.
- Add the green chilli-ginger paste and reserve.
- Put the oil in a large pan of about 2-litre capacity. When hot, add the mustard seeds and let them crackle.
- Add the asafoetida powder or garlic, curry leaves and green chilli. Once the leaves crackle (almost immediately), pour in the yoghurt mixture.
- Stir in the turmeric powder and the cooked beans with the remaining cooking

water.
- Add salt to taste, bring to a boil and then reduce to a simmer.
- Gently mash some of the beans against the wall of the pan to give body to the dish. Taste and adjust salt and the consistency if required.
- Garnish with coriander leaves and serve hot with steamed rice.

Turiya Shaak
(Ridged Gourd Stew)

This is another simple home-style preparation of my mother's that I love. Traditionally served as a vegetable, it can also pass off as a chunky soup. For best results, cook this just before serving and do not cover while cooking. I like to eat it with just steamed rice.

Time: 20 minutes | Serves: 3-4

Ingredients
- 1 kg ridged gourd (toori)
- 1 tbsp oil
- ½ tsp asafoetida powder (hing)
- ½ tsp mustard seeds
- 1-2 green chillies, slit
- 1 tsp sodium bicarbonate
- Salt to taste

Method
- Peel the gourds, cut them into half and then into 1" pieces.
- Put the oil in a pan on medium heat. When hot, add the asafoetida powder and mustard seeds. When the seeds crackle, add the green chillies and the gourd.
- Stir in the sodium bicarbonate.
- Add salt to taste and 1 cup of water and cook uncovered or cover with water on the lid. (This spreads the heat and when the water is reduced, it means the food is cooked.)
- Cook, till the gourd is tender and has let out its juices.

Kairi Ni Chutney
(Green Mango Chutney)

One of the most piquant chutneys ever! It is great with everything — khichdi, dal-rice, and even roti.

Time: 20 minutes | Makes: 300 gms of chutney

Ingredients
- 250 gms raw green mangoes
- Grated jaggery, half the volume of the mangoes
- 2 tsp red chilli powder
- 1 tsp cumin seeds
- Salt to taste

Method
- Wash the mangoes and dry thoroughly. Peel and chop the flesh. Measure the volume of mangoes in cups.
- Place everything in a food processor and blend to a coarse purée, adding a little water, if required.
- Taste and adjust seasoning, adding more jaggery if you want it sweeter.
- Transfer to a serving bowl.
- This chutney will last over a week, refrigerated.

Cheese Soup

I love this soup Mom makes. Each vegetable contributes a world of texture and flavour. I even like to use a concentrated purée of this soup as a substitute for cream or white sauce in other soups and pasta dishes.

Time: 40 minutes | Serves: 4

Ingredients

Vegetables

- 200 gms bottle gourd (lauki/ghia/doodhi), chopped
- 200 gms cauliflower, chopped
- 2 medium-sized potatoes, chopped
- 200 gms cabbage, chopped
- 2 small onion, chopped

White sauce

- 2 tbsp butter or olive oil
- 2 tbsp refined flour (maida)
- 300 ml milk, at room temperature
- 1 cup grated Cheddar cheese

Garnish (optional)

- 1 tbsp grated Cheddar cheese
- A handful of croutons

Method

- Put the vegetables in a pressure cooker with 2 cups of water and pressure-cook for 7-10 minutes on low heat, after the cooker reaches full pressure.
- Remove from heat and set aside, till cool.
- Purée the cooked vegetables in a blender (there is no need to strain this soup) and reserve. To make the white sauce, heat the butter or olive oil gently in a heavy-bottomed pan.
- Add the flour and stir to combine, ensuring there are no lumps. Cook, till the

flour darkens and releases a nutty aroma.
- Remove the pan from heat and pour in the milk, stirring vigorously to ensure that no lumps are formed.
- Return the pan to low heat and cook, till the mixture thickens enough to coat a wooden spoon.
- Stir in the cheese and allow it to melt.
- Mix in the puréed vegetables and bring to a boil.
- Adjust the consistency to your liking, cooking longer if you want it thicker or adding milk or stock to thin it down.
- Garnish with grated cheese and serve the croutons on the side with garlic bread and a salad.

Variation: *You can use a 50:50 ratio of tofu and cheese to garnish.*

Tips: *For a quicker version I combine the butter or olive oil, flour and milk in a pan, mix till smooth and place on low heat to cook, stirring all the while.*

Mom's House Salad

Mom loves salads and this is a simple recipe she tosses together almost daily.

Time: 30 minutes | Serves: 4

Ingredients

Dressing

- 2 tbsp olive oil
- 1 tbsp balsamic vinegar
- 2 garlic cloves, crushed
- ½ tsp sugar1 tsp Italian dried herb mix or oregano
- ½ tsp freshly ground pepper
- Salt to taste

Salad

- 1 head of iceberg lettuce, washed and leaves torn to bite-size
- 1 cup cherry tomatoes, halved
- ½ cup carrot shavings (use a peeling knife to shave fat ribbons)
- ½ cup diced yellow bell pepper
- ½ cup diced cucumber
- ½ cup corn kernels, boiled

Method

- Combine all the ingredients for the dressing, mix well and set aside.
- Combine all the ingredients for the salad and toss well. Refrigerate, till ready to serve.
- When ready to serve, toss again with the dressing.
- Transfer to a bowl and serve.

Cauliflower Or Okra Tempura
(A Chindian meal, Mom style!)

This happens to be another of my mother's signature recipes. It's most definitely a crowd-pleaser, and fabulous when accompanied by some of Mum's Spice of Life (page 56)!

Time: 30 minutes | Serves: 6-7

Ingredients

- 1 kg cauliflower, cut into florets or 1 kg okra (bhindi), sliced into large chunks on the diagonal
- ½ cup arrowroot flour
- ½ cup cornflour
- ½ tsp sodium bicarbonate
- 4 green chillies, coarsely ground
- 1 tbsp ginger-garlic paste
- 1 tbsp salt
- Oil for deep-frying

Method

- If using the cauliflowers, blanch them for 1 minute in boiling salted water, drain and set aside. Combine both the flours in a large bowl with the sodium bicarbonate and mix well.
- Add the green chillies, ginger-garlic paste and salt and mix again.
- Put the oil in a frying pan on medium heat.
- When hot, add the vegetable to the flour mix and toss well to ensure the pieces are well coated.
- Fry the vegetable in small batches, till golden and crisp on the outside.
- Drain on kitchen paper and serve immediately.

Schezwan Potatoes

Time: 20 minutes | Serves: 4-8

Ingredients
- 1 kg potatoes
- 3 tbsp oil
- ½ cup sliced spring onion bulbs and tender greens
- ½ cup chopped green bell pepper
- ½ cup spice of life chutney (page 56)
- ½ cup tomato purée
- Salt to taste
- Freshly ground black pepper powder

Garnish
- 2 tbsp sliced spring onion bulbs and tender greens

Method
- Wash the potatoes, peel and cube them. Boil them in just enough water to cover, till tender but firm. Drain.
- Put the oil in a pan on medium heat. When hot, add the remaining ingredients, except the potatoes. Mix, till well blended.
- Add the cooked potatoes.
- When the sauce sticks to the potatoes, take the pan off the heat.
- Taste and adjust seasonings.
- Transfer to a serving platter.
- Garnish with spring onions, insert toothpicks into some of the potatoes and serve while still warm.

Sweet Corn Soup

Time: 20 minutes | Serves: 4

Ingredients
- 5 tbsp cornflour
- 5 cups vegetable or chicken stock or water
- 1 cup canned cream-style sweet corn
- 1 tsp freshly ground white pepper
- 1 tsp sugar
- 1 tsp soy sauce
- Salt to taste

Method
- Mix the cornflour with ⅓ cup of water.
- Boil the stock or water in a pan on high heat.
- Reduce the heat and add the corn, pepper, sugar, soy sauce and salt to taste. Stir well and simmer uncovered for about 3 minutes.
- Turn the heat to high, add the cornflour mixture and stir continuously, till the soup thickens. Simmer for a minute.
- Serve with chilli sauce and green chillies in vinegar.

Variations
- *For an egg version, beat one egg and drizzle it into the boiling soup in a thin stream.*
- *For a chicken or crab version, add ¼ cup of cooked chicken or crab to the soup just 2 minutes before you take it off the heat.*

Aubergine In Sweet-Sour Sauce With Spring Onions

Time: 30 minutes | Serves: 4

Ingredients

- 1 kg long, thick aubergines (baingan)
- 3 tbsp + 1 tbsp oil
- 6 garlic cloves, chopped
- 100 gms spring onion bulbs and tender greens, finely chopped

Sweet-sour sauce

- ½ cup white wine vinegar
- ½ cup sugar
- ½ cup tomato ketchup
- 1 tbsp cornflour
- 1 tsp red chilli sauce
- 1 tbsp soy sauce
- 1 tsp coarsely ground black pepper
- Salt to taste

Garnish

- 2 tbsp finely chopped spring onion bulbs and tender stems
- Freshly ground black pepper

Method

- Cut the aubergines lengthwise into quarters. Remove and discard the seeds. Cut the aubergine flesh into 2" pieces.
- Put 3 tbsp of oil in a frying pan on medium heat. When hot, fry the aubergines for about 2 minutes. Remove and drain on kitchen paper.
- Combine all the sauce ingredients in a pan with 1 cup of water. Put the pan on medium heat and simmer, till thick.
- Heat 1 tbsp of oil in another pan and sauté the garlic and spring onions.
- Add the aubergines and pour in the sauce. Cook for one minute.
- Serve garnished with spring onions and black pepper.

Fried Rice

Time: 30 minutes | Serves: 4

Ingredients
- 1½ cups long-grained rice
- ½ tsp salt + to taste
- 1 medium-sized carrot, diced
- 12 French beans, diced
- 4 tbsp oil
- 2 spring onion bulbs and tender greens, diced
- ½ cup tiny cauliflower florets
- 1 small green bell pepper, diced
- 4 tbsp soy sauce
- 100 gms spring onion greens, chopped

Method
- Wash the rice and drain.
- Boil 1 litre of water in a large pan on high heat. Add the rice and ½ tsp of salt and cook uncovered on medium heat, stirring occasionally, till the rice is tender but firm. Ensure that the grains are separate and don't clump up.
- Drain the cooked rice and allow to cool completely.
- Blanch the carrot and French beans in boiling salted water for 1 minute each.
- Put the oil in a wok on high heat. When hot, stir-fry the spring onions and cauliflower for 1 minute.
- Add the carrot, French beans and bell pepper and stir-fry for 2 minutes.
- Stir in the rice, soy sauce and spring onion greens. Mix well ensuring that the rice is not broken.
- Add salt to taste.
- Taste and add more salt, if required.
- Stir-fry on high heat for 3-5 minutes, remove and serve.

Sweet And Sour Vegetables

Time: 30 minutes | Serves: 4

Ingredients
- 1 carrot, cut into medium slices
- 16 French beans, cut into 1" pieces
- 1 tbsp oil
- ¼ cup cauliflower florets
- 1 medium-sized cucumber, cut in ½" pieces
- 1 small green bell pepper, cut in ½" pieces
- 2 medium-sized tomatoes, finely sliced
- 1 cup chopped pineapple
- 2 spring onion bulbs and tender greens, sliced lengthwise into quarters
- Salt to taste

Sweet and sour sauce
- 1 cup tomato sauce or ketchup
- ½ cup white wine vinegar
- 4 tbsp sugar
- ½ tsp freshly ground white pepper
- 3 tbsp cornflour

Method
- Blanch the carrot and French beans in boiling salted water for 1 minute each. Drain and set aside.
- Put the oil in a wok on high heat. When hot, stir-fry the cauliflower for about 2 minutes.
- Add the carrots, French beans, cucumber and bell pepper. Stir-fry on high heat for about 3 minutes, till tender but crunchy.
- Add the tomatoes and remove from heat.
- Combine the tomato sauce, vinegar, sugar, pepper and 1½ cups of water in another pan. Put it on high heat and bring to a boil while stirring well.

- Mix the cornflour with ½ cup of water and pour it into the sauce, stirring continuously. Simmer on medium heat for about 2 minutes.
- Add the cooked vegetables, pineapple, spring onions and salt to taste.
- Simmer for a minute and serve.

Hakka Noodles

Time: 20 minutes | Serves: 4

Ingredients
- 400 gms noodles
- 1 tbsp oil
- 2 tsp chopped garlic
- 3-4 dried red chillies, broken into pieces
- 1 cup shredded cabbage
- 1 cup julienned green bell pepper
- 1 cup sliced spring onion bulbs and tender greens
- 2 tbsp chilli oil
- Salt to taste

Method
- Cook the noodles according to the instructions on the package, till al dente.
- Put the oil in a wok on medium heat. When hot, add the garlic and red chillies and stir-fry for a few seconds.
- Add the vegetables and cook on high heat for about 2 minutes.
- Stir in the noodles, chilli oil and salt to taste. Mix well and cook for another minute.
- Serve hot.

Lost Recipes

I made spinach soup for the first time in thirteen years on the day I wrote this chapter. And I made it exactly as my father liked it. Just like I procrastinated making the soup, I postponed the writing of this chapter. This has been the hardest to write in this book. Not because I didn't know what to write — there was a lot — but for once, the words would not come.

Twelve years ago, I lost him. Suddenly and quickly, while we were on the most idyllic holiday in South Africa. It was the best trip of our lives, almost as though he wanted to leave us with the best memories of himself. There had been an increasingly bittersweet air to things as we did them all that last week, and statements he made came back. His warm hug a couple of days into our trip when I missed Shekhar (my boyfriend at the time, and so sore a point that we never spoke of him) and Dad's quiet affirmation, 'Why don't you enjoy me while I am here, you will have the rest of your life with him?' And then when I was crying a few days later for some silly reason, his exasperated question, 'Why must you cry every time? You have to learn to face odds, I will not always be there to protect you!' and then that last night, at dinner, as we finished the soup course (spinach soup) he turned around and said, 'This is good, but not as good as yours, you make the best spinach soup.' His last words to me.

That day, as I made my spinach soup again, I reflected on just how many of the memories I had of him revolved around food. Perhaps because when my usually aloof Dad cooked, he stepped out of the role of the authoritarian and into a more approachable persona; food seemed to melt barriers that he used to keep the world out. As on days when dakkho was made by Pratima Foi or Mom's Indian Chinese was on the menu. He would give us kids rare glimpses of him as a family man. If the women in my life set the bar on home cooking, my father, HBM as he was called, introduced my palate to all sorts of flavours I would never have tasted at home. Our family was strictly vegetarian, even eggs were not allowed in the main kitchen (because Maharaj, our Brahmin cook, would not tolerate it). He believed that we should learn to eat everything; so in spite of my grandmother's decree against it and my mother's frantic protests, he took us out to restaurants at every opportunity and encouraged us to eat non-vegetarian. And thanks to him I can remember, even today, the precise moment when my palate awoke! It was with the first spoonful of the hot and sour soup at the Radio Club.

Typical as it was for men of his time he cooked to impress, BBQ on weekends with friends, or a rare meal when we went on holiday. And yet the dish I remember him for most was a simple fried rice. It was on perhaps the only occasion ever when it was just the two of us at home, because Mom was travelling and my siblings were at boarding school. He got it into his head to make fried rice. I've never really been able to remember what he did, but I remember it was a hot sticky, spicy, mess as far away from fried rice as I knew it! And it was delicious. I scarfed down two helpings and effusively praised it because I was thrilled to be the sole focus of so much of his attention and secretly hoped my response would elicit more of the same.

It did.

For the next month, Dad made the same fried rice for me.

E-v-e-r-y s-i-n-g-l-e D-A-Y!!!

My initial enthusiasm for platefuls soon waned. Reducing to a single serving and then even less, till I couldn't bear to eat another bite! Unable to communicate my revulsion for fear of hurting his feelings, I gave up and religiously ate a plateful every day, till my mother mercifully returned. A few months later Dad passed away and I wish I had had that third plateful while I had the chance. Whenever I remember it, I crave it to the point of pain.

Dad was not a good cook by any measure. And I don't have a recipe for his fried rice. I wish I did. But I suspect even if I did, I could never quite recapture its flavour; the exact proportion of big fat vegetables to sticky rice, the blend of sauces he poured in down to the drop, or get the balance of undercooked vegetables to scorched rice exactly right. Lost recipes are like lost moments. You never get them back.

Spinach Soup

This started out as a soup, but over time it has evolved into a great multi-purpose recipe — as the base for a soup, an all-purpose sauce to toss pasta or anything in, or to add fortification to sandwich fillings, roti dough or mashed potatoes.

Time: 25 minutes | Serves: 3-4

Ingredients
- 1 kg spinach
- 1 tbsp butter or olive oil
- 150-200 gms onions, sliced
- 4 garlic cloves, minced
- Pasta water or home-made stock for thinning the soup
- 250 gms freshly cooked noodles, pasta or potatoes

To serve
- ½ cup freshly grated Parmesan cheese

Method
- Wash the spinach thoroughly in several changes of water.
- Blanch the spinach in boiling salted water for 1 minute, till it just wilts and turns bright green. Drain, squeeze dry and chop coarsely.
- Put the butter or olive oil in a pan on medium heat. When hot, add the onions and sauté, till translucent.
- Add the garlic and sauté for about 1 minute.
- Mix in the spinach and stir-fry for another minute. Remove from heat and cool.
- Blend the spinach to a purée, using a little pasta water or stock to thin it, if required.
- Return the purée to the pan and reheat gently.
- Add the cooked noodles, pasta or potatoes. Stir well, so that it is well coated and serve warm with grated Parmesan on the side.

Amiri Khaman
(Bengal Gram Snack)

This was my Dad's favourite farsan. I remember the first time I had it because he taught me how to assemble it and fed it to me with so much glee!

Time: 1 hour 10 minutes + 6 hours for soaking + 4 hours to rest | Serves: 8-10

Ingredients
- 450 gms husked, split Bengal gram (chana dal)
- 6 green chillies, roughly chopped
- 1" piece of fresh ginger, roughly chopped
- 1 tsp sodium bicarbonate
- ½ tsp turmeric powder
- 1 tsp salt or to taste
- 3 tbsp powdered sugar
- Juice of 2 large limes

Tempering
- 4 tbsp oil
- 2 tsp mustard seeds
- 20 garlic cloves, finely chopped
- ¼ tsp asafoetida powder (hing)

Garnish
- 2 tbsp finely chopped coriander leaves
- 2 tbsp grated fresh coconut
- 2 cups gram flour strings (sev)

Method
- Wash the dal and soak it in water for at least 6 hours.
- Drain and reserve 4 tbsp.

- Grind the rest with the green chillies and ginger.
- Add the reserved dal with the sodium bicarbonate, turmeric powder and 1 tsp of salt to the ground dal. Mix well and set aside for at least 4 hours.
- Spread a little mixture at a time in a thali and steam for 10 minutes, to make dhoklas. The batter should be dry in the centre and the surface shiny. Test by inserting a knife into the centre; it should come out clean.
- Cool and crumble.
- Add the sugar and lime juice and mix well.
- Taste and add more salt, if required.
- Put the oil for the tempering in a small pan on medium heat. When hot, add the mustard seeds. When they crackle, add the garlic and asafoetida powder and fry for a few seconds.
- Pour the tempering over the crumbled dhoklas.
- Garnish with coriander leaves, coconut and sev and serve.

Tip: *You can also use ready nylon khaman dhokla to make this dish.*

Ivy Gourd Moong Dal Salad

This recipe is dear to me because I associate it with my father. One Sunday afternoon, he entered the kitchen to make it. I never forgot the rare experience of seeing that side of him.

Time: 20 minutes + 4 hours for soaking | Serves: 4

Ingredients
- ½ cup husked, split moong beans (moong dal)
- 1 cup finely chopped ivy gourd (tindora)
- 1 green chilli, finely chopped
- ½ tsp red chilli powder
- A pinch of salt, or to taste
- Juice of 1 lime

Garnish
- 2 sprigs coriander leaves, finely chopped
- 1 tbsp grated fresh coconut

Method
- Wash the dal and soak it in water for about 4 hours.
- Drain and rinse the dal and place it in a mixing bowl.
- Add the gourd, green chilli, chilli powder, salt and lime juice and toss well.
- Sprinkle over with the coriander leaves and coconut and serve.

Dakor Na Gota
(Spicy Gram Flour Fritters)

This speciality from the village of Dakor in Gujarat was my father's favourite pakoda recipe.

Time: 45 minutes | Serves: 4

Ingredients
- 1 cup gram flour (besan)
- ½ cup semolina (rava/sooji)
- 1 tsp green chilli-ginger paste (see note on page 11)
- 1 tsp cumin seeds
- ½ tsp turmeric powder
- ½ tsp garam masala powder
- ½ tsp red chilli powder
- 1 tsp fennel seeds (saunf)
- 1 tsp coriander seeds
- 1 tbsp sesame seeds (til)
- 1 tbsp whole black peppercorns
- ¼ tsp sodium bicarbonate
- 2 tbsp sugar
- ½ tsp citric acid crystals or 1 tsp lime juice
- ½ cup water
- 2 tbsp chopped coriander leaves
- Salt to taste
- 3 tbsp oil + extra for deep-frying

Method
- Combine all the ingredients except the oil for deep-frying in a mixing bowl with ½ cup of water and make a batter. Allow the batter to stand for 15-20 minutes.
- Put the oil for deep-frying in a kadhai or wok on medium heat. When hot, reduce the heat to low and stir the batter vigorously.

- Drop spoonfuls of batter into the hot oil and fry small pakodas on gentle heat so that the insides are cooked well.
- Drain on kitchen paper and serve hot with a sweet chutney.

Nairobi Butter Tava Prawns

Whenever we travelled to Nairobi, my father would carry a large bag of a special consignment for the men of the Mediratta family, with whom we stayed. King prawns on dry ice. And the very same day, there would be a men's night by the poolside where these would be slow-cooked on a three-inch tava or griddle over a charcoal fire.

Time: 30 minutes + 30 minutes for marination | Serves: 6-7

Ingredients
- 1 kg king prawns, off the shell
- 125 gms fresh ginger, grated
- 250 gms garlic, chopped
- 1 tsp turmeric powder
- ½ tsp salt or to taste
- 500 gms butter
- 1 tbsp cracked black peppercorns
- ½ cup chopped green chillies, or to taste
- ½ cup chopped coriander leaves
- Juice of 2 limes

Garnish
- Lime slices
- Finely chopped green chillies

Method
- Clean the prawns, devein and wash well. Drain and pat dry.
- Combine 1 tbsp each of the ginger and garlic with the turmeric powder and salt in a large bowl and mix well.
- Add the prawns and mix, till well coated. Set aside to marinate for 30 minutes.
- Melt the butter on a tava or griddle. Add the peppercorns, green chillies and the rest of the ginger and garlic and stir-fry, till fragrant.

- Add the prawns and cook, till they just curl up and turn pink.
- Sprinkle the coriander leaves and lime juice over the prawns.
- Serve the prawns with lime slices and sprinkle green chillies on top to add a splash of colour.

Phirni
(Rice Custard)

Every year at Ramzan, my father would visit Muhammad Ali Road in Mumbai to get his fill of all the fabulous food to be found there during that time. And we knew he had been when we woke up to kulhads of phirni in the refrigerator, redolent of rose water and the terracotta containers it was set in.

Time: 40 minutes + 4 hours for soaking + 4 hours refrigeration | Serves: 4

Ingredients
- 1 cup rice
- 1 tbsp almonds
- 1 tbsp pistachios
- ½ cup + 1 litre milk
- 6-8 tbsp sugar
- 1 tsp green cardamom powder
- A few saffron strands

Garnish
- 1 sheet silver leaf (varq)
- A few rose petals

Method
- Wash the rice and soak it in water for 4 hours.
- Soak the almonds and pistachios in hot water for a few hours, till they swell and their skins slide off. Peel them and slice fine.
- Drain the rice and grind it with ½ cup of milk in a food processor to a semi-fine consistency.
- Put 1 litre of milk in a pan of 3-litre capacity on high heat. Add the sugar and cardamom powder.
- Once the milk is hot, reduce the heat to the minimum and gradually stir in the

ground rice paste. Keep stirring continuously, to prevent the rice from becoming lumpy and burning.
- Add the saffron strands and cook on very low heat, stirring continuously, till the milk thickens to the consistency of a custard.
- Once the milk has been soaked up and the rice is cooked to tenderness (taste a little to make sure), add half the almonds and pistachios.
- Remove from heat and allow it to cool.
- Divide the phirni into bowls, preferably earthen (kulhads). These lends a lovely flavour to the phirni.
- Decorate with the remaining nuts, sliver leaf and rose petals.
- Refrigerate for at least 4 hours before serving. The longer the phirni sits in the earthen bowls, the better it tastes.

Pratima Foi's Dakkho
(A Slowly Simmered Vegetable Stew Enriched with Pulses and Legumes)

I inherited this recipe from my bua (maternal aunt) Pratima Parikh and it is close to my heart because it has so many memories attached. My father loved this dish and whenever my Foi visited, dakkho would be on the menu at least once. We'd go to the market to buy the vegetables and then pile them on the large dining table. Everyone would congregate around to help cut them or just chat over endless cups of chai supplied by our long-suffering Maharaj, who would then cook up a huge cauldron of it. It uses all of the vegetables and leafy greens available in the season. The recipe calls for three pulses and legumes but I actually use handfuls of all the dals I have in my kitchen.

Time: 2-3 hours + overnight for soaking | Serves: 8-12

Ingredients
- 1 cup husked, split pigeon peas (toover/arhar dal)
- 1 cup husked, split Bengal gram (chana dal)
- 50 gms potato
- 50 gms cauliflower
- 50 gms cabbage
- 50 gms ivy gourd (tindora)
- 50 gms okra (bhindi)
- 50 gms green peas
- 50 gms carrot
- 50 gms French beans
- 50 gms fresh black-eyed beans (lobia)
- 50 gms aubergine (baingan)
- 50 gms bottle gourd (lauki/ghia/doodhi)

- 50 gms snake gourd (chirchinda)
- 50 gms bitter gourd (karela)
- 50 gms spiked gourd (kantola)
- 50 gms elephant yam (suran)
- 50 gms sweet potato (rataloo)
- 50 gms cucumber
- 50 gms field beans (papdi)
- 50 gms white radish
- 50 gms ridged gourd (toori)
- 50 gms karonda (Carissa congesta)
- 100 gms spring onion bulbs and tender greens
- 100 gms red amaranth leaves (chauli)
- 100 gms spinach
- 5-6 colocasia leaves (more if small)
- 100 gms fresh dill leaves (sua)
- 100 gms coriander leaves
- 100 gms white radish leaves
- 50 gms fresh green pigeon peas (toover/arhar)

Tempering
- ½ cup ghee
- ½ cup oil
- ½ tsp mustard seeds
- ½ tsp cumin seeds
- ½ tsp aniseed (saunf)
- 2-3 onions, finely chopped
- 1 whole garlic bulb, peeled and finely chopped
- 1 tbsp ginger paste
- A lime-sized ball of tamarind without seeds and fibres
- Lime juice to taste
- Green chillies to taste, finely chopped
- Salt to taste

Method

- Wash the dals and soak them in water overnight.
- Rinse and pressure-cook the dals with just enough water to cover for 12 minutes on low heat, after the cooker reaches full pressure.
- Remove from heat and set aside, till the pressure subsides.
- Transfer to a bowl and reserve.
- Clean, wash and cut all the vegetables into medium dice.
- Clean and wash all the leaves thoroughly in several changes of water. Drain and chop them.
- Pressure-cook all the vegetables, leaves and the green pigeon peas with just enough water to cover for 8 minutes on low heat, after the cooker reaches full pressure.
- Remove from heat and set aside, till the pressure subsides.
- Put the ghee and oil in a large pan on medium heat. When hot, add the mustard seeds, cumin seeds, aniseed, onions and garlic.
- When the onion turns golden, add the ginger, the cooked dals and vegetables and tamarind.
- Mix well and bring to a boil.
- Add lime juice, salt and chillies to taste. Mix well and bring to a boil again.
- Serve hot with puris in the traditional manner or hot buttered pao, as I do.

Maharaj

Considering my roots (I am half Gujarati and half Kutchi), I recently realised that my knowledge, or rather lack thereof, of Gujarati food was appalling. As long as there were moms, aunts and a host of other friendly Gujjus around to feed me, I had taken it for granted that we would always be provided for! But when I moved away, first to boarding school and then to my own home after I married, I missed and craved the food I grew up eating. And Maharaj, with his vast knowledge about Gujarati food was the ideal teacher.

Maharaj (cooks who usually come from Rajasthan are called Maharaj out of respect for their Brahmin lineage), Chandra Shekhar Mehta, has been with and cooked for my family since I was born. He was not a culinary teacher in the direct sense but several dishes I craved for and learnt to cook as a result of those cravings, are ones he cooked and were, in essence, my first introduction to them.

Maharaj turned out to be a font of information on food in general and especially so on Gujarati cuisine. It was from him that I learnt that the Gujarati food that my friends laughed at for being sweet, actually aimed to strike a balance of flavours. An element of sweetness was added in the form of jaggery or gud, but it was to bring out the other flavours. So when tasting food, a Gujarati cook will often ask if the khattash (sourness) or mithash (sweetness) is correct. Thanks to Maharaj's knowledge, our family was exposed to a much larger variety of Gujarati food than just that of our region. Maharaj continues to be a cornerstone of the culinary history of my family, the living repository of generations of women from my grandmother down to my daughter. A cook of all stripes, he can produce everything from traditional Gujarati food to Chinese, Italian and a few things even I do not know, with an élan that would put master chefs to shame. He still always has a kind word for me and gives my husband the deference he would extend to a son-in-law. And as he did for me as a child, he always has a little treat for my kids today: a lump of jaggery, a fistful of nuts or a few chunks of cucumber if he is cutting a salad, or ever so often, a box of mohanthal, something nobody on earth makes as well as him.

Gujarati Dal Dhokli
(Lentils with Wheat Flour Dumplings)

This was a weekend special we really loved as children, and Maharaj still makes it the best. Here is his recipe. You can precook the dal and also make the dough in advance.

Time: 25 minutes | Serves: 6

Ingredients

Dhokli

- 200 gms wholewheat flour (atta)
- 1 tsp salt
- 1 tbsp turmeric powder
- 1 tsp carom seeds (ajwain)
- 2 tbsp red chilli powder
- 2 tbsp oil

Dal

- 250 gms husked, split pigeon peas (toover/arhar dal)
- 1 tbsp tamarind, without seeds or fibre
- 1 tbsp jaggery dissolved in 1 tbsp water
- 50 gms shelled peanuts
- 1 tbsp garam masala powder
- 1 tsp red chilli powder
- 1 tsp turmeric powder
- 2 small tomatoes, chopped
- Salt to taste

Tempering

- 2 tbsp ghee
- 3-4 cloves
- 2 x 1" cinnamon sticks
- 1 tbsp mustard seeds

- 1 sprig curry leaves
- 3 green chillies
- A pinch of asafoetida powder (hing)

Garnish
- ½ cup finely chopped coriander leaves

Method

Dhokli
- Sift the flour into a bowl.
- Add the salt and spices and mix well.
- Add the oil and mix it into the flour.
- Knead the mixture into a dough of roti-like consistency, gradually adding up to ½ cup of water. Set aside.

Dal
- Wash the dal and pressure-cook it with 3 cups of water for 5-7 minutes on low heat, after the cooker reaches full pressure.
- Remove from heat and set aside, till the pressure subsides.
- Put the ghee for the tempering in a pan on medium heat. When hot, add the whole spices.
- When they crackle, add the curry leaves, green chillies and asafoetida powder.
- Pour the tempering over the dal.
- Put the tamarind, dissolved jaggery and 2 cups of water in a bowl and mix, till well blended. Add the peanuts and spice powders and mix well.
- Pour the contents of the pan into the dal.
- Add the tomatoes and salt to taste. Simmer on low to medium heat, till the tomatoes disintegrate.

To complete the dish
- Roll the dhokli dough into large rotis and cut them into diamond shapes.
- Bring the dal to a boil and add the dhoklis. Boil for 10 minutes and remove from heat.
- Garnish with coriander leaves and serve immediately with finely chopped onions, lime wedges and melted ghee on the side.

Methi Dal Dhokli
(Lentils with Fenugreek-stuffed Wheat Flour Dumplings)

Later on, when I started cooking at home, my finicky Mommy side concluded that dal dhokli missed out on fibre. So I developed a recipe for a stuffed dal dhokli inspired by ravioli. Use this for a heartier version of the dish above by substituting these stuffed versions for the plain dhoklis used.

Time: 1 hour | Serves: 4-6

Ingredients

Dal

- 250 gms husked, split pigeon peas (toover/arhar dal), cooked and tempered as given for Gujarati dal dhokli (page 93)

Dough

- ½ cup wholewheat flour (atta)
- ½ tsp red chilli powder
- ¼ tsp turmeric powder
- 2 tsp oil
- ½ tsp salt

Filling

- 1 large potato
- ½ cup fenugreek leaves (methi)
- 1 green chilli, finely chopped
- ¼ tsp garlic paste
- ¼ tsp red chilli powder
- Salt to taste

Garnish

- ½ cup finely chopped coriander leaves
- 2 tbsp melted ghee

Method

Dough

- Sift the flour for the dough into a bowl. Mix in all the remaining dough ingredients.
- Knead to make a soft dough using water as required.
- Cover and set aside.

Filling

- Boil the potato, till tender. Peel and mash it.
- Pluck out the fenugreek leaves and wash them thoroughly in several changes of water. Drain well.
- Mix all the filling ingredients together in a bowl.
- Taste and add more salt if required. Reserve.

To assemble the dhokla

- Take a lemon-sized ball of dough in your palm, and roll out into a ¼" thick disc.
- Use a round, small cookie cutter to cut out circles 2" in diameter.
- Place a little stuffing in the centre of each circle. Fold the edges of the circle over the stuffing to form a ball. Flatten the ball into a disc.
- Continue, till all the dough and filling are used up.
- To complete the dish
- Cook the dal as given for Gujarati dal dhokli and temper it.
- Add the dumplings to the boiling dal. Boil for 15 minutes and remove from heat.
- Garnish with coriander leaves, sprinkle with ghee and serve immediately with finely chopped onions and lime wedges on the side.

Makai Ni Khichdi
(Spicy Corn Curry)

This is a luscious, spicy way to cook corn. I like it on white toast.

Time: 30 minutes | Serves: 2-3

Ingredients
- 2 cups tender corn kernels, grated off the cob or crushed in a mixer
- 1 cup milk, diluted with ⅓ cup water
- 1 tsp green chilli paste
- 1 tsp ginger paste
- 1 tsp sugar
- Salt to taste
- ¾ tbsp lime juice

Tempering
- 2 tbsp oil
- ½ tsp mustard seeds
- ½ tsp turmeric powder

Method
- Combine the corn with the diluted milk, green chilli and ginger pastes and sugar in a pressure cooker. Stir well and add salt to taste.
- Pressure-cook the corn for 10-12 minutes on low heat, after the cooker reaches full pressure.
- Remove from heat and set aside, till the pressure subsides.
- Put the oil for the tempering in a large pan on high heat. When hot, add the mustard seeds. When they start to crackle, add the turmeric powder.
- Add the cooked corn.
- Mix well, reduce the heat to medium and let the corn simmer. If it seems too dry, you can add some water or milk.
- Remove, add the lime juice and mix well.
- Serve hot.

Coconut Curry

This is my mother's recipe, one she invented by combining recipes for a Maharashtrian curry and a Parsi dhansak. But Maharaj adapted to it very well and it became a regular on our menus, often served for dinner on Sundays.

Time: 45 minutes | Serves: 4-6

Ingredients

Dal

- 3¾ tbsp husked, split moong beans (moong dal)
- 3¾ tbsp husked, split Egyptian lentils (masoor dal)
- 3¾ tbsp husked, split pigeon peas (toor/arhar dal)
- 1¼ tbsp whole black gram (sabut urad)

Spice powder

- 7-8 dried red Kashmiri chillies
- 3 tbsp coriander seeds
- 5 whole black peppercorns
- 3-4 cloves
- 1 bay leaf

Coconut paste

- 1 tbsp oil
- 4-6 medium-sized onions, chopped
- ½" piece of fresh ginger, chopped
- 8-10 garlic cloves, chopped
- 3 green chillies, chopped
- 1 fresh coconut, grated

Curry

- 6-7 tomatoes, chopped

- 1 tbsp oil
- 1½ tbsp cumin seeds
- ½ tsp red chilli powder
- ½ tsp turmeric powder
- 1 tsp curry powder (commercial)
- 1 tsp salt, or to taste
- Juice of 1 lime

Method

Dal

- Wash the dals and put them into a pressure cooker. Add water to cover and pressure-cook for 10-12 minutes on low heat, after the cooker reaches full pressure.
- Remove from heat and set aside, till the pressure subsides.

Spice powder

- Roast the red chillies, whole spices and bay leaf on a dry tava or griddle on low to medium heat, till fragrant; be careful not to scorch them.
- Cool and grind to a fine consistency. Reserve.

Coconut paste

- Put the oil for the coconut paste in a small pan on medium heat. When hot, add the remaining ingredients, except the coconut. Sauté, till well browned.
- Remove from heat and cool.
- Grind to a fine paste with the coconut. Reserve.

Curry

- Put the tomatoes in a pan and cook on medium heat for 7-8 minutes, till soft and mushy. Cool and purée the tomatoes in a blender. Reserve.
- Put the oil in a pan on medium heat. When hot, add the cumin seeds.
- When they crackle, add the coconut paste and fry, till the oil separates.
- Add the spice powders and ground spice powder and fry again, till aromatic. Sprinkle in some water if required to prevent burning.
- Add the cooked dal and bring to a boil.
- Stir in the puréed tomatoes and salt, mix well and bring to a boil.
- Remove from heat and sprinkle in the lime juice.
- Serve with steamed white rice, fried onions and lime wedges on the side.

Mohanthal
(Gram Flour Fudge)

Time: 1½ hours + 2½ hours for setting | Makes: 2 kg of fudge

Ingredients
- 100 ml milk
- 200 gms + 600 gms ghee
- 1 kg gram flour (besan)
- 1¼ kg + 250 gms sugar
- A few saffron strands
- 400 gms khoya/mawa (unsweetened milk solids), crumbled
- ½ tsp freshly grated nutmeg

Garnish
- A few sheets of silver leaf (varq)

Method
- Mix the milk and 200 gms of hot ghee with the gram flour in a bowl.
- Sift it through a wide-meshed sieve into a fresh bowl.
- Combine 1¼ kg of sugar with 1¼ litres of water in a pan and bring to a boil on high heat.
- Boil, till the syrup is of a 2-string consistency. (Place a little of the cooled syrup between your thumb and forefinger, and open them gently; two strings should be formed.)
- Add the saffron and set aside.
- Heat the remaining ghee in a pan and add the gram flour mixture. Roast it on low to medium heat, till slightly brown.
- Remove from heat and cool to room temperature.
- Add the sugar syrup, khoya and nutmeg and mix well.
- After about 5 minutes, pour the mixture into a thali.
- After about 30 minutes, gently place the silver leaf on the mohanthal, and after 2 hours, cut into pieces.

Cornflake Chivda
(Cornflake Snack)

Time: 15 minutes | Makes: 1 kg of chivda

Ingredients
- 2 tbsp oil
- 250 gms cornflakes
- 100 gms peanuts
- 100 gms husked, split roasted Bengal gram (bhuna chana dal)
- 100 gms cashewnuts, broken
- 100 gms powdered sugar
- 1 tsp dried mango powder (amchur)
- 1 tsp red chilli powder
- Salt to taste

Method
- Put the oil in a wok on low heat. When hot, add the cornflakes and fry for a few seconds.
- Add the peanuts, dal and cashewnuts and fry for a further minute.
- Stir in the remaining ingredients.
- Taste and add more salt, if required.
- Remove from heat and cool.
- Store in a clean, dry airtight jar.

Vatana Na Ghugra
(Green Pea Fritters)

Time: 2 hours | Makes: 100 pieces

Ingredients

Dough

- 3 kg refined flour (maida)
- 3 tsp salt
- 1 tbsp oil

Filling

- 1 kg green peas
- 200 gms coriander leaves
- 1 tbsp oil
- 1 tsp asafoetida powder (hing)
- 100 gms green chilli-ginger paste (see note on page 11)
- 1 tbsp lime juice, dried mango powder (amchur) or citric acid crystals
- 20 gms beaten rice (poha)
- 400 gms fresh coconut, grated
- Salt to taste

To cook the fritters

- Oil for deep-frying

Method

Dough

- Sift the flour and salt into a bowl.
- Add the oil and rub with your fingertips, till it resembles breadcrumbs.
- Add water, a little at a time and knead to make a firm dough. Set aside.

Filling

- Shell the green peas and crush them lightly. Reserve.
- Wash the coriander leaves in several changes of water. Drain well and chop

fine. Reserve.
- Put the oil in a kadhai or wok on medium heat. When hot, add the asafoetida powder.
- Add the crushed green peas and cook for about 5 minutes.
- Stir in the remaining filling ingredients and mix well.
- Taste and add more salt, if required.

To assemble and cook the fritters
- Pinch off walnut-sized balls of dough and roll them out into rotis on a lightly floured surface.
- Spread 2 tsp of filling along one half of each roti, keeping the edges of the roti free.
- Fold the other half over the filling and pinch the edges together to seal.
- Put the oil for deep-frying in a kadhai or wok on medium heat. Fry the fritters in batches, till golden brown.
- Drain on kitchen paper and serve hot with green chutney.

Sev Tameta Nu Shaak
(Gram Flour String And Tomato Curry)

Time: 30 minutes | Serves: 4-6

Ingredients
- 2 tsp oil
- ½ tsp cumin seeds
- ½ tsp mustard seeds
- ½ tsp asafoetida powder (hing)
- 1 green chilli, chopped
- 1 small onion, chopped
- ½ tsp grated ginger
- 3 medium-sized tomatoes, chopped
- 1 tsp garam masala powder
- ½ tsp cumin powder
- ½ tsp turmeric powder
- Salt to taste
- 120 gms gram flour strings (sev)

Method
- Heat the oil in a kadai. Add the cumin seeds, mustard seeds, asafoetida powder and green chilli. When the mustard seeds crackle, add the onion and ginger.
- Sauté, till the onion turns light brown and the oil starts to separate out.
- Add the tomatoes, garam masala, cumin powder, turmeric powder and salt to taste.
- Add in 1 cup of water and cook with a lid on the kadai for about 10 minutes, until the tomatoes have dissolved into a gravy.
- Remove from heat.
- About 5 minutes before serving, top with sev and serve hot with parathas or rotis.

Tip: *You can add ½ tsp of sugar to cut the sourness of the tomatoes.*

Trikona Puri
(Triangular Deep-fried Puffed Flatbreads)

Maharaj makes these the best. They were my favourite snack when I was a child. In fact, even now, when they arrive for my children, I usually give in to the temptation of scarfing down a few with ketchup!

Time: 1½ hours | Makes: 1¼ kg puris

Ingredients
- 1 kg refined flour (maida)
- 2 tsp salt
- 2 tbsp nigella seeds (kalaunji)
- 100 gms ghee
- Oil for deep-frying

Method
- Sift the flour and salt into a bowl. Mix in the nigella seeds.
- Add the ghee and rub with your fingertips, till it resembles breadcrumbs.
- Add water, a little at a time and knead to make a loose but firm dough.
- Divide into equal-sized balls.
- Roll each ball out into a circle on a lightly floured surface.
- Fold in half and then into a quarter to form small triangles.
- Put the oil for deep-frying in a kadhai or wok on medium heat. Fry the puris in batches, for about 5 minutes, till golden and crisp.
- Drain on kitchen paper and store in clean, dry airtight jars.

Fada Ni Khichdi
(Moong and Broken Wheat Medley)

One of the snacks that were made on Uttarayan or Makar Sankranti, the harvest festival — a day looked forward to with great excitement by our family.

Time: 1 hour | Serves: 6-8

Ingredients
- 1 cup husked, split moong beans (moong dal)
- 4 cups broken wheat (dalia)
- 3 tbsp ghee
- 1" cinnamon stick
- 3 cloves
- 1 tsp cumin seeds
- ½ tsp asafoetida powder (hing)
- 1 cup diced potatoes
- 1 cup shelled green peas
- 1 cup cauliflower florets
- 1 cup diced onions
- 1 tbsp green chilli-ginger paste (see note on page 11)
- ½ tsp whole black peppercorns
- ½ tsp turmeric powder
- 1 tsp red chilli powder
- Salt to taste

Method
- Wash the dal and broken wheat and soak them in water for at least 15 minutes. Drain and reserve.
- Bring 4 cups of water to a boil and reserve.
- Put the ghee in a pressure cooker on medium heat. When hot, add the

cinnamon, cloves, cumin seeds and asafoetida powder and sauté for about 30 seconds.
- Add the dal, broken wheat and remaining ingredients. Stir well for 4-5 minutes.
- Pour in the hot water and pressure-cook for 10 minutes on low heat, after the cooker reaches full pressure.
- Remove from heat and set aside, till the pressure to subside.
- Open and stir the cooked khichdi vigorously, adding a little hot water, if required so that the dal and the broken wheat mix well.
- Serve hot.

Fada No Sheero
(Broken Wheat Dessert)

Time: 1 hour | Serves: 8

Ingredients
- ¼ cup ghee
- ½ cup broken wheat (dalia)
- ¼ cup seedless raisins and almond slivers
- ⅓ cup sugar
- ½ tsp green cardamom powder

Method
- Melt the ghee in a kadhai or wok on medium to low heat. Add the broken wheat and cook, stirring frequently, till it changes from pale brown to a reddish brown.
- Add the raisins and almonds.
- Pour in 2 cups of boiling water. Stir well and cover the pan with a lid. Keep the heat low and cook for about 10 minutes, stirring periodically, till the wheat has soaked up all the water and looks fluffy.
- Add the sugar and cardamom powder and mix well. Cook for 5 minutes longer.
- Remove from heat, cool and refrigerate.
- Serve cold.

Discovering the Kitchen

One of my earliest memories is of standing up on a kitchen stool, stirring anything I was allowed to. I always hounded my Mom or Maharaj (the family cook) with: 'Can I do that, can I do that?' I don't think it was the cooking that I wanted to do so much initially; I think I just wanted to be like the women I had grown up watching.

My grandmothers, my mother and the other women in my sphere of existence cooked because they had to, of course. But they also cooked because they loved the people they cooked for. It didn't matter when you came in, the first thing they would say was, 'Have you eaten? Can I get you something?' The first time I remember cooking by myself was when I wanted to make a chocolate cake. I had watched Mom make it a thousand times and just replicated the order of mixing things. And then thought I was brilliant because I baked it within minutes in the microwave! My cousin, Ashubhai, was very kind and said it was wonderful. How he got that piece of rock down his throat I have no idea! You see, while I mixed things the way my mother used to, at the age of nine, I had no idea that one needed to follow something called a recipe!

And then there was the time I tried to replicate the chocolate mousse we learned at school. Anyone who has made a mousse will tell you that the egg whites need to be beaten to stiff peaks; something I had achieved at school but that would just not happen at home no matter how much I beat them! At the home science class at school, we learned about recipes but it just never occurred to the novice cook I was, that multiplying a recipe by ten to cater to my huge family would skew proportions somewhat. It took Mom's expertise to salvage litres worth of chocolate-flavoured egg and milk mix into something akin to ice cream! But every cloud has a silver lining and my culinary disasters must have made Mom aware of the fact that I would not be deterred from cooking. So a few days later, my mother spent a lovely afternoon guiding me through making a sweet potato pie out of a cookbook I had brought home from the school library. I was using a cookbook for the first time and it was a lesson in following recipes and measurements! The next day I managed the perfect scrambled eggs on my own. And then my mother let me have a free hand in the kitchen.

I didn't really do much with the freedom, save for perfecting the scrambling of an egg and being ready to do it for anyone, any time. But I must have absorbed some cooking skills by osmosis along the way, because they came to the fore on my brother's sixteenth birthday (I would have been about eighteen by then). A big party was planned for him. The guests had all arrived but the cooking was yet to begin! Luckily all the preparations had been made and I don't know what drove me but that day but I successfully cooked an entire meal for twenty-five people single-handedly! And it brought rave reviews from everyone.

After that, I was hooked! I was a shy child who had grown into a bookish introvert as a teenager. Cooking got me appreciation and helped me gain confidence. Recipes became my maps to building self confidence. But now, when I knew I had cooked well that kind of feedback was addictive. I constantly created new milestones for myself by trying my hand at more complex recipes and the more my cooking was appreciated, the more I wanted to cook! Even today, I need the rush that appreciation of my cooking gives me.

The women of the house were not required to cook daily so I did not really learn to cook traditional food. So till I married, my culinary prowess was limited to a handful of 'special' meals of cheesy 'baked dishes', rich soups, exotic salads and the Indian Chinese food I learned from my mother, of course. But I think the fact that most of the cooking I did at that point was hobby cooking made a big difference to the future cook I would be. I wonder if I would have developed as adventurous an attitude to cooking if I had been trained in traditional cooking at that point.

Keema Pasta

Keema Pasta was a wicked combination of pasta and dense, grainy, spicy keema that was an occasional feature of the Friday 'Conti food night' at Mayo. And this keema pasta — the unholy result of spaghetti bolognaise corrupted with spices and silky 'Bambino' macaroni (not healthy durum wheat pasta touted as proper these days, but the maida version that reduces to a stodgy mess if overcooked) — is the reason why the finest spaghetti bolognaise pales in comparison for me even today.

Time: 1 hour | Serves: 6-8

Ingredients
- ½ cup ghee
- 2-3 cloves
- 1" cinnamon stick
- 5-6 whole black peppercorns
- 2 green chillies, chopped
- 500 gms onions, finely chopped
- 1 kg mutton, minced
- 1 tsp ginger-garlic paste
- ½ tsp red chilli powder
- ½ tsp turmeric powder
- 1 tsp garam masala powder
- 500 gms tomatoes, finely chopped
- Salt to taste
- 500 gms pasta, cooked (page 150)

Garnish
- 1 cup coriander leave

Method

- Put the ghee in a large, heavy-bottomed pan on medium heat. When hot, add the whole spices, green chillies and onions. Stir-fry, till the onions have lost all their moisture and are well browned.
- Add the mince and stir to break up the lumps as it cooks.
- Add the ginger-garlic paste, and stir-fry, till it has released all its juices. Keep cooking, till dried out. At this point, your mince will be crumbly and well on its way to browning.
- Mix in the spice powders, reduce the heat and stir-fry, till fragrant.
- Add the tomato, mix well and cook, stirring occasionally, till the tomatoes disappear and the ghee rises to the surface.
- Add salt to taste. Your keema should be slightly saltier than you like because the pasta will come in.
- Add the previously cooked pasta and mix well. (This is where a big pan comes in handy because things begin to fall out otherwise.)
- Cover and cook for a few minutes. Open and a fragrant cloud of steam, laden with aromas will rise up – awesome!
- Wash the coriander leaves thoroughly in several changes of water. Drain well and chop fine.
- Spoon the pasta in a serving dish, top with the coriander leaves and serve. You can serve it with bread and a salad on the side, but I never bother, because nobody touches anything else once the pasta is served.

Masoor Dal
(Husked, Split Egyptian Lentils)

Time: 1 hour | Serves: 4

Ingredients

- 1 cup husked, split Egyptian lentils (masoor dal)
- ½ tsp turmeric powder
- 1 tbsp finely chopped ginger
- 2 tsp salt
- 2 tbsp ghee
- ⅛ tsp asafoetida powder (hing)
- 1 tsp cumin seeds
- ½ cup finely chopped onions
- ½ cup finely chopped tomatoes
- 1 tsp coriander seeds, powdered
- ½ tsp red chilli powder
- ½ tsp garam masala powder
- Salt to taste

Garnish

- 2 tbsp chopped coriander leaves

Method

- Wash the dal and put it in a heavy-bottomed pan with 3 cups of water, the turmeric powder, ginger and salt. Place the pan on high heat, partially covered, and cook, till tender.
- Put the ghee in another heavy-bottomed pan on medium heat. When hot, add the asafoetida powder and cumin seeds.
- When they begin to crackle add the onions. Sauté, till they turn brown.
- Mix in the tomatoes and stir-fry, till the ghee separates and rises to the surface.
- Add the spice powders, mix well and cook, till fragrant.

- Pour the contents of the pan over the dal.
- Add salt to taste.
- Bring to a boil, then simmer for about a minute.
- Garnish with the coriander leaves and serve hot.

Kofta Curry

We got these once a week, with lobia and rotis at Mayo. For some reason rice was never served those days. I would mash the two together and eat the mix by the spoonful with rolled up rotis. It's a combination I have never eaten again, but every time I eat lobia dal I remember that meal combination. The koftas in this dish can be made with minced mutton or chicken.

Time: 1 hour | Serves: 4-6

Ingredients

Kofta

- ½ cup coriander leaves
- 1 kg mutton, minced
- 2 onions, very finely chopped
- 2 tbsp garlic paste
- 3 tbsp ginger paste
- 2 tbsp garam masala powder
- 1 tsp salt

Curry

- 3 tbsp vegetable, canola or sunflower oil
- 3 onions, very finely chopped
- 1 tbsp ginger paste
- 2 tbsp garlic paste
- 2 tsp coriander powder
- 1 tsp cumin powder
- ½ tsp turmeric powder
- 1 tsp red chilli powder
- 1 tsp garam masala powder
- 4 large tomatoes, cubed

- Salt to taste

Garnish
- 2 tbsp chopped coriander leaves

Method
Kofta
- Wash the coriander leaves thoroughly in several changes of water. Drain well and chop fine.
- Put all the kofta ingredients in a large bowl and mix well.
- Form spoonfuls of the mixture into walnut-sized balls and reserve.

Curry
- Put the oil in a pan on medium heat. When hot, and add the onions and sauté, till they are light brown.
- Add the ginger and garlic and stir-fry for a minute.
- Sprinkle in the spice powder and stir-fry for 2-3 minutes.
- Add the tomatoes and mix well. Fry, till the oil begins to separate and rises to the surface.
- Pour in 2 cups of warm water and season with salt to taste. Bring to a boil.
- When it boils, gently add the koftas. Do not stir for at least the next 5 minutes.
- Then give the dish a gentle stir to avoid breaking the koftas.
- Simmer uncovered, till the koftas are cooked and the gravy has the desired thickness. Transfer to serving bowl, garnish with coriander leaves and serve hot.

Lobia
(Black-Eyed Beans)

Time: 1 hour + overnight for soaking the beans | Serves: 4

Ingredients
- 2 cups black-eyed beans (lobia)
- 1 tsp salt
- 1½ tsp red chilli powder
- 1½ tsp coriander powder
- ¾ tsp cumin powder
- ½ tsp turmeric powder
- 2 tbsp oil1 small onion, chopped
- ¾" piece of fresh ginger, chopped
- 2 large garlic cloves, chopped
- ½ tsp cumin seeds
- 1 medium tomato, chopped

Method
- Wash the beans and soak them in water overnight.
- Drain the beans and rinse thoroughly.
- Put them into a pan, cover with fresh water and bring to a boil on high heat.
- Add the salt and spice powders. Simmer on medium heat, for 30-45 minutes, till the beans are just tender.
- Put the oil in deep pan on medium heat. Add the onion, ginger, garlic and cumin seeds and sauté for about 10 minutes.
- Mix in the tomato and cook for another 5 minutes.
- Add the beans along with the cooking liquid and simmer uncovered, till the beans are soft but not completely dissolved. The dish should be soupy.

Railway Tomato Soup

Time: 45 minutes | Serves: 6

Ingredients

- 1 kg tomatoes, chopped
- 1 small carrot, chopped
- 1 turnip, chopped
- 2 onions, chopped
- 2 tsp salt
- 1 tsp sugar
- 1 tsp freshly ground black pepper

Garnish

- Oil for deep-frying
- 2 slices bread, cubed
- 3 tbsp cream

Method

- Put all the vegetables in a pan with the salt and 1 cup of water on high heat. Cover partially and bring to a boil.
- Reduce the heat and simmer, till the vegetables are completely cooked through. Remove and set aside, till cool enough to handle.
- Pass the vegetables through a soup strainer or blend in a blender and then strain into a fresh pan.
- Add enough water to make 4½ cups of liquid.
- Put the pan on high heat and bring to a boil.
- Reduce heat and add the sugar and pepper. Simmer for about 10 minutes.
- While the soup is simmering, heat the oil for the croutons in a small frying pan and fry the bread cubes, till brown and crisp.
- Remove and drain on kitchen paper.
- Serve the hot soup garnished with swirls of cream and the croutons on the side.

Mayo Mutton Curry

Time: 1½ hours | Serves: 4

Ingredients

Spice paste

- 2 tbsp ghee
- 6 curry leaves
- 1" piece of fresh ginger, chopped
- 6 garlic cloves, chopped
- 6 dried red chillies, broken
- 2 medium-sized onions, chopped
- 1 tbsp coriander seeds
- 1 tsp cumin seeds
- ½ tsp turmeric powder

Curry

- 2 tbsp ghee
- 500 gms mutton on the bone, cut into 1" pieces
- 2 potatoes, cut into 1" cubes
- 1 tsp salt
- 4 cups mutton stock or water
- 1 cup tomato purée
- 2 tbsp chopped coriander leaves

Method

Spice paste

- Put the ghee in a pressure cooker on medium heat. When hot, add the curry leaves, ginger, garlic, red chillies and onions and sauté for 2-3 minutes, till fragrant.
- Cool and set aside.
- Roast the coriander seeds and cumin seeds on a dry tava or griddle on medium heat, till fragrant.

- Combine the sautéed and roasted ingredients with the turmeric powder and grind to make a fine paste, adding a little water as required.

Curry

- Put the ghee in the same pressure cooker on medium heat. When hot, sauté the mutton pieces for 2-3 minutes.
- Add the ground spice paste and sauté for 3-4 minutes longer.
- Stir in the potatoes.
- Add the salt and stock or water and mix.
- When it comes to a boil, stir in the tomato purée and coriander leaves.
- Close the cooker and pressure-cook for 10 minutes on low heat, after the cooker reaches full pressure.
- Remove from heat and set aside, till the pressure subsides.
- Serve hot.

Mayo Chicken Curry

Served on Tuesdays with roomali roti

Time: 1½ hours | Serves: 4

Ingredients
- 4 tbsp oil
- 2 cloves
- 1" cinnamon stick
- 2 black cardamom pods
- 1 tsp cumin seeds
- 1 onion, chopped
- 1½ tbsp chopped ginger
- 6 garlic cloves, chopped
- Salt to taste
- ½ tsp turmeric powder
- 1 tbsp coriander powder
- ½ tsp red chilli powder
- 2 tomatoes, puréed
- 450 gms chicken, skinned and jointed
- ½ tsp garam masala powder
- 2 tbsp chopped coriander leaves

Method
- Put the oil in a large non-stick pan on medium heat. When hot, add the whole spices and fry for about 20 seconds, till aromatic.
- Add the onion and sauté for about 10 minutes, till golden brown.
- Stir in the ginger and garlic and cook, stirring all the while, for about 40 seconds.
- Add a pinch of salt and the spice powders and stir for 15 seconds.
- Pour in the puréed tomatoes and cook on medium heat for about 10 minutes, till the liquid in the pan has dried and the oil leaves the sides of the masala.

- Add the chicken and brown on medium to high heat for 3-4 minutes.
- Pour in just enough water (about 350 ml) to cover the chicken.
- Add salt to taste.
- Bring to a boil, reduce the heat to low and simmer, till the chicken is cooked through. The slower it cooks the better it tastes. This takes about 15 minutes for small joints and up to 25-30 minutes for larger ones. Check with a fork.
- Stir in the garam masala powder and coriander leaves and serve with rice or rotis and raita or any vegetable dish.

Spicy Potato Pinwheels

Thankfully the Mayo cake came after my time! So this was the first thing I ever cooked at Mayo. I cooked it along with my classmate Purnima Singh for our Home Science examination in Class 8. The recipe was given to us by Ma'am Singh, the matron for Sanyogita house at that time. It has been a part of my repertoire ever since and I find it quite surprising that many of my friends and relatives have never heard of it.

Time: 1 hour | Serves: 4-6

Ingredients

Dough

- 1 cup flour
- 1 tbsp cornflour + extra for rolling
- 2 tbsp ghee

Filling

- 1 cup coriander leaves
- 4-5 potatoes
- ½ tsp garam masala powder
- 2 tsp roasted cumin powder
- 2-3 tsp green chilli-ginger paste (see note on page 11)
- Salt to taste

To fry the pinwheels (optional)

- Oil for deep-frying

Method

Dough

- Sift the flour and cornflour into a bowl. Add the ghee and rub with your fingertips, till it resembles breadcrumbs.
- Add chilled water, a little at a time and mix to make a semi-firm dough.

- Knead well, till it has the consistency of a roti dough. Cover and set aside while you prepare the filling.

Filling
- Wash the potatoes and boil them, till tender. Cool, peel and mash them. Reserve.
- Wash the coriander leaves thoroughly in several changes of water. Drain well and chop fine.
- Combine all the filling ingredients in a bowl and mix well. Taste and adjust the seasonings.

To assemble and cook the pinwheels
- Roll out the dough on a surface lightly dusted with cornflour, till quite thin, turn it over a couple of times, so that it doesn't stick to the surface.
- Spread the filling carefully over the rolled out dough leaving about ½" around the edges free.
- Wet the edges with a little water and starting at one end, roll the dough tightly into a cylinder. Seal the edges well.
- With a sharp knife slice the roll into 1" thick horizontal slices (straight or on the diagonal).
- If you want to fry the pinwheels, heat the oil in a kadhai or wok and deep-fry on medium heat, till golden brown.
- Alternatively, bake them in an oven preheated to 180°C for 10-12 minutes. Turn over and bake, till golden brown.
- Serve hot with green chutney or tomato ketchup.

Neha's Twist On Mayo Cake: Chocolate Balls

The recipe I got from the girls when I visited was: Crush one week's worth of biscuits of the whole Mayo dormitory (some sacrifices have to be made) and mix with one bottle of Horlicks, stolen from the mess. Add whatever else you can find to this potent mix (coke works!) and water and mix everything together on the floor and eat with a wooden ruler for maximum enjoyment. Thankfully, my sister Neha sent me a more refined version with this note.

'Dear Di, I was thinking about your book and just remembered how the first form of cooking food we ever learnt was kacchha Maggi and Mayo cake. I am not sure if you have this recipe, but I am giving you my improved one...'

Time: 45 minutes | Makes: 20-30 chocolates

Ingredients

- 1 large packet Marie biscuits
- 50 gms drinking chocolate powder
- 150 ml condensed milk
- 1 cup powdered desiccated coconut

Method

- Crush the biscuits into fine granules and place them in a bowl.
- Add the drinking chocolate powder and condensed milk. Mix well.
- Add a little water if needed.
- Roll the mixture into small balls and then roll in the desiccated coconut to decorate.

Mayonnaise

I discovered mayonnaise when I stayed with my aunt in Singapore at the age of sixteen. I took to it with a vengeance, my favourite snack being white bread slathered with Kraft Mayonnaise. When I returned to India, I just could not find one that matched in flavour. Then one day, Winnie Aunty, my mother's secretary, told me how to make it. After I discovered home-made mayo, there was no way I was going back to the store-bought stuff. Over time, I also began to do variations, like the pickled mayo which went down very well. Here are the recipes.

Time: 30 minutes | Makes: 250 gms

Ingredients
- 1 tbsp sugar
- 1 tbsp hot mustard powder
- Juice of 1 lime
- 1 tsp salt
- 1 egg
- 500 ml oil

Method
- Put the sugar, mustard, lime juice and salt in the blender and give it a whiz.
- Add the egg and blend to incorporate it.
- Keeping the blender on low speed, pour in the oil in a slow, steady stream.
- The mayonnaise will begin to thicken as the oil is added. The more oil you add, the thicker your mayonnaise will get.
- After about 100 ml has been incorporated, stop and check the consistency. If you are happy with it, your mayonnaise is ready. If not then continue to add oil, till you reach the consistency you like.

Variations: For a pickled version, chop 2 green bell peppers and 2 onions fine. Place in a bowl with vinegar to cover and poach for a while or microwave. Cool and stir it into the mayonnaise.

Carrot And Onion Soup With Parsley Oil

This soup was born of an experiment, after I bought parsley home, but realised it was too different from coriander leaves as a substitute. The soup turned out so delicious, it stayed. I usually make extra parsley butter, slather baguette slices with it and grill them. You could also make cheese chilli melts with parsley butter instead of regular butter or oil.

Time: 1 hour | Serves: 4

Ingredients

- 1 tbsp butter or olive oil
- 6 garlic cloves, crushed
- ½ tsp freshly ground black pepper
- 1 cup finely sliced carrots
- 1 cup finely sliced onions
- 2 tbsp refined flour (maida)
- 6 cups vegetable or chicken stock
- ½ tsp salt

Parsley butter

- 2 tbsp butter
- ½ cup parsley, finely minced

Method

- Put a deep, heavy-bottomed pan on high heat, till hot. Reduce the heat and add the butter or oil.
- Add the garlic and stir-fry, till golden.
- Sprinkle in half the pepper.
- Add the carrots and stir-fry gently for about 3 minutes, till the colour brightens.
- Mix in the onions and stir-fry for another 3 minutes, till they turn translucent.

- Add the flour and continue to stir-fry, till the vegetables are well coated.
- Cover the pan, reduce the heat to the minimum and allow the vegetables to sweat, stirring occasionally, till they give out their juices and the same have been absorbed by the flour. When you uncover the pan it should be fragrant.
- Pour in the stock and stir well.
- Add the salt and remaining pepper. Raise the heat to high and bring to a boil. Continue, to boil, till the soup thickens.
- To make the parsley butter, place a small pan on low heat. When hot, add the butter. When it bubbles, add the parsley, swirling the pan to combine. Allow the parsley to crisp up slightly in the butter for about a minute and pour the contents of the pan over the soup.

13-onion Pasta

This is yet another kitchen experiment that stayed. Over the years, I have bought the fanciest knives, but I always gravitate back to the ten-rupee knife from Bhuleshwar my grandmother introduced me to. The thing cuts like a dream! I call this the 13-onion pasta for want of a better name because the first time I made it, I used thirteen onions, chopping each slowly but precisely into tiny dice. I always love vegetables chopped just right. I am downright finicky about it and that knife was such a pleasure to use, that I could not stop, till I had chopped up all the onions around — thirteen of them. I do not use thirteen onions any longer, but the name stuck. And much later, I found that this combination of onion, carrot and celery was a classic mirepoix, the triumvirate of ingredients that is the base of French cooking!

Time: 1 hour | Serves: 4

Ingredients

- ½ cup butter or olive oil
- 4-5 cloves
- 1 tbsp freshly crushed black pepper
- 1 bay leaf
- 1 tbsp ginger-garlic paste
- 1 cup finely chopped carrots
- 1 cup finely copped onions
- 1 cup finely copped celery
- ½ tsp salt
- 200 gms cooked pasta such as fusilli or farfalle
- ½ cup pasta cooking water

Garnish

- ½ cup grated Cheddar cheese

Method

- Put the butter or oil in a large pan on medium heat. When hot, add the spices and bay leaf and sauté for 1 minute, till the butter or oil is infused with their flavours. Mix in the ginger-garlic paste.
- Add the carrots, onions and celery and stir well. Cook on low heat, till the vegetables are soft and cooked through.
- Sprinkle in the salt and mix well.
- Add the cooked pasta and the cooking water and stir well again (the pasta water will moisten the pasta and spread the flavours of the vegetables).
- Serve hot, topped with grated cheese.

Spicy Layered Vegetable Casserole

This recipe was inspired by a 'baked dish' my aunt Archana Munshaw made for me when I was very young. I always loved it because it combines colourful layers of vegetables. I have used the same elements of carrot, spinach, buttery mashed potatoes and creamed corn, but smothered it all in a sweet chilli tomato sauce to suit adult palates.

Time: 1 hour | Serves: 4

Ingredients

Sauce

- 2 tbsp butter
- 1/3 tsp sugar
- 6 garlic cloves, finely chopped
- 1 small onion, finely chopped
- 1 tbsp Kitchen King masala powder
- 3 medium-sized tomatoes, blanched, peeled, seeded and puréed
- 1 tsp salt

Casserole

- 2 cups salted cooked potatoes, mashed with butter
- 1 cup salted cooked carrots, mashed with ½ tsp mustard
- 1 cup puréed spinach
- 1 cup sweet corn cream-style (from a can)
- 1 cup grated Cheddar cheese

Method

Sauce

- Melt the butter in a large pan on low heat. Add the sugar and stir, till it dissolves.
- Add the garlic and onion and sauté, till fragrant.

- Sprinkle in the Kitchen King masala powder and sauté for 20 seconds, till fragrant.
- Stir in the puréed tomatoes and bring to a boil on high heat.
- Add salt, reduce the heat to a simmer and cook, till the butter rises to the surface.
- Remove and set aside.

To assemble and bake the casserole
- Oil a baking dish lightly and spread a thick layer of potatoes on the base.
- Top with a layer of carrot, followed by spinach and the creamed corn.
- Pour the sauce over the vegetables and top with grated cheese. Cover the dish with foil.
- Bake in an oven preheated to 200°C for 15 minutes.
- Remove the foil and continue to bake uncovered for 10 minutes, till the cheese is light brown.
- Serve hot.

Marble Cake With Raisins And Cherries

I discovered baking with a vengeance when I was in Singapore after my ICSE board examinations, which is when I created this variation of the marble cake. It has stuck!

Time: 1 hour 20 minutes | Serves: 6-8

Ingredients

- 225 gms butter at room temperature + extra for greasing
- 225 gms refined flour (maida) + extra for dusting
- 225 gms castor sugar
- 4 eggs, whisked
- 2 tsp vanilla extract
- 2 tsp baking powder
- 50 ml milk
- 50 gms cocoa powder, sifted
- 50 gms seedless raisins
- 50 gms glace cherries, halved

Method

- Butter an 8" round cake tin and dust it lightly with flour. Line the tin with greaseproof paper.
- Cream the butter in a large bowl or an electric food mixer, till soft.
- Add the sugar and beat, till the mixture is light and fluffy and has paled to an off-white shade.
- Whisk the eggs and vanilla extract together in a small bowl and add it to the butter mixture a little at a time, beating well between each addition, till the egg is well incorporated.
- Sift the flour and baking powder into a bowl and fold it gently into the mix.
- Add the milk and mix gently to combine.
- Divide the batter into 2 portions.
- Into one half, fold the sifted cocoa powder and raisins.

- Into the other half, mix in the cherries.
- Pour spoonfuls of the 2 portions alternately into the prepared cake tin.
- Using a skewer or similar implement, gently draw swirls through the cake mixture to 'marblise' it. Try not to over-mix or you won't get the marble effect.
- Place in an oven preheated to 180°C and bake for 45 minutes or till a skewer inserted into the centre comes out clean.
- Turn the cake out on to a wire rack and allow to cool before serving.

Chilli Cheese Melts

Chilli cheese toast was one of the first things I started to make for myself. But like all classic template recipes, it has travelled with me through my life. Versatile enough to put together just about anywhere, it made great quick breakfasts on work-day mornings. Over the years I learned to vary the cheeses to glam up this dish.

Time: 10 minutes | Serves: 2-4

Ingredients
- 1 cup grated cheese
- 1-2 green chillies, finely minced
- 8 slices white bread
- Butter or olive oil

Method
- Combine the cheese and green chillies in a bowl and mix well.
- Spread a little butter or olive oil on each bread slice.
- Sprinkle the cheese mixture on 4 slices. Cover with the other 4 slices to make sandwiches. Set aside.
- Cook the sandwiches on both sides on a tava or griddle on medium heat or put them under a medium grill, till the outsides are crisp and golden and the cheese has melted.
- Serve with hot masala chai for extra kick!

Some variations I have tested
- Cheddar cheese and finely chopped jalapeños.
- Parmigiano Reggiano with green peppercorns and olives.
- Cumin Gouda with green chillies.

The First Dance

When Shekhar and I decided to marry, everyone thought I was making a mistake and had to let me know! Family, friends, the corner grocer, my beautician, everyone was into the 'enlighten Rushina' movement. Their trump card: 'You don't even know how to cook, how are you going to run your home?'

'They didn't know that, at the table, Shekhar and I had understood each other a long time ago. In our year in hostel, we had discovered we were both happy to make the long journey to Reshmi Dhaba in Secunderabad for our favourite meal of chunky, ginger-spiked hot and sour soup and succulent tandoori chicken. I'd even learned to cook dal and rice from him by then.

It was also the year that Shekhar passed the 'will stay by your side through everything test'! Like the time I thought I was doing something really brilliant by making chilli con carne with the South African biltong Mom brought back from one of her trips. All I did was substitute the beans with chickpeas, eliminate the wine and use biltong (which is dried meat jerky) instead of meat. Yep, that's all I did, honest. It was summarily flushed down the loo. Over the next few months several hurdles were overcome: our families came together and the date arrived. Before we knew it we were headed back to a life as husband and wife in our new apartment in Mumbai. Shekhar left for work the very next morning and I embraced my new life with a vengeance.

I now had my own kitchen! The first thing I did was to provision it. Only, coming from a large family of twenty, I didn't know how to do anything in small quantities and ordered enough groceries to last six months! I had stuff falling on my head for weeks afterwards! When I was done arranging my new kitchen, I found I had little handfuls of various pulses and lentils left over. On a whim, I decided to make dal kababs as a special dinner that night. Entirely from my imagination! Thankfully they turned out well and the first dinner I made for my husband was a success. He still loves those kababs but I cannot believe how cheesy I was! That day, my indulged childhood ended, I had crossed a threshold into my adult life. As long as I was single, I never thought about my meals. Now the responsibility for meals, the RDBS (roti-dal-bhaat-subzi) I had once groaned over, became mine. Those first months were an adventure as I juggled learning to run a kitchen, commute two hours both ways to work across town every day and manage a home.

There were the disasters of the early married years — the week of the purple pasta, for instance. Never ever add red cabbage to anything unless you want purple results! And there were the cheese pebble cookies that turned out hard as rocks, and the Thai curry that burnt our innards so bad we had to eat yoghurt for a week!

But with time, I learned to cook for two. I also learned tips and tricks from women around me that let me optimise time and cook quickly and efficiently. I planned menus and devised routines, chopped and prepped on Sundays, so I would have to just toss a few things together for a salad or pasta, or temper a dal through the week. I became the 'one-dish wonder', extremely proficient at cooking meals that required just one bowl to cook and serve in (it meant less dishes to wash at the end of a the long days we both had).

Kumi Bhabhi-inspired Hearty Mexican Bean Dip

My sister-in-law Isha Shah, who we all know as Kumi bhabhi, is an amazing cook. One of the things she is famous in the family for is her Mexican taco spread which she made for my laadka laddu. This is her recipe, with a few touches added by me over the years.

Time: 30 minutes | Serves: 4

Ingredients
- 1 tbsp olive oil
- 1 medium-sized onion, chopped
- 4 garlic cloves, chopped
- 1 tsp brown sugar
- 1 tbsp wine vinegar
- 1 tsp toasted cumin powder
- 1 tsp red chilli powder
- 1 tsp dried oregano
- 1 cup mixed beans, cooked
- 2 medium-sized tomatoes, coarsely chopped
- Salt to taste

Garnish
- ⅓ cup grated Cheddar cheese

Method
- Put the oil in a pan on medium heat. When hot, fry the onion and garlic, till soft.
- Add the sugar, vinegar, spice powders and oregano and cook for 1 minute.
- Add the mixed beans and tomatoes. Simmer for 10-15 minutes, till thick.
- Season with salt to taste.
- Transfer to a serving bowl. Scatter grated cheese on top and serve with tacos or tortilla chips.

Neelu Bhabhi's Chole Bhature

Neelu bhabi is my late cousin Ashubhai's wife. She is brilliant at many things, and quite a perfectionist in the way she does them, but she has one problem: she hates to cook. Back when the Munshaws still lived together as a joint family, the daughters-in-law of the house sometimes split kitchen duty when Maharaj took leave. On one such occasion, Neelu bhabhi made chole bhature. I have never forgotten how good it was!

Time: 1½ hours + overnight for soaking the chickpeas | Serves: 2

Ingredients

Bhature

- 2 cups refined flour (maida)
- ½ tsp baking powder
- 1/3 cup yoghurt, whisked smooth
- 1 tsp sugar
- ¾ tsp salt
- 300-400 ml oil for frying

Chole

- 1½ cups garbanzo beans/chickpeas (Kabuli chana)
- 1 large tomato
- 1 tsp ghee or oil
- ¾ cup chopped onions
- ½ tsp ginger-garlic paste
- ½ tsp red chilli powder
- 1 tsp dried fenugreek leaves (kasoori methi)
- Rock salt to taste

Spice powder

- 1 green cardamom pod

- 2-3 cloves
- ½ tsp coriander seeds
- ½ tsp cumin seeds
- ¼ tsp fenugreek seeds (methi)
- 3-4 whole black peppercorns
- ½ tsp rock salt

Garnish
- 2-3 sprigs coriander leaves, chopped

Method

Bhature
- Mix all the ingredients, except the oil, to form a smooth dough and keep it aside for an hour.
- Take small amounts of the dough and roll them into balls.
- Roll the balls into a disc of the desired size for the bhatura.
- Heat the oil in a kadhai or wok and deep-fry the bhature when you are ready to eat.
- Drain them on kitchen paper before serving.

Chole
- Soak the beans in water overnight.
- Drain and rinse thoroughly.
- Pressure-cook the beans with enough water to cover for 25-30 minutes on low heat, after the cooker reaches full pressure.
- Remove from heat and set aside, till the pressure subsides.
- The beans should be cooked through and easily flattened when pressed.
- If you are using canned beans, wash them 2-3 times. Reserve.
- Blanch the tomato in hot water, till the skin is wrinkled. Peel and blend into a smooth purée.
- Roast the spice powder ingredients on a dry tava or griddle on medium heat, till fragrant. Cool and grind to make a fine powder.
- Put the ghee or oil in a pan on medium heat. When hot, fry the onions and ginger-garlic paste, till the onions turn slightly brown.
- Add the puréed tomato, the roasted and ground spice powder and chilli powder. Sauté for 2-3 minutes.

- Add the cooked beans, fenugreek leaves and salt to taste and cook for another 5 minutes.
- Garnish with coriander leaves.
- Serve hot with bhature.

Note: *For more gravy, you can increase the tomato and onions.*

Dal Kababs

I'd say it's mandatory to make these heart-shaped for full flavour!

Time: 45 minutes + overnight for soaking the dals | Serves: 4-6

Ingredients
- 1 cup mixed dals in equal proportions (whatever you have on hand)
- 1 tbsp grated ginger
- 2 tbsp finely chopped garlic
- 2 tbsp finely chopped green chillies
- 2 tbsp gram flour (besan)
- 2 tbsp finely chopped coriander leaves
- ½ tsp red chilli powder
- ½ tsp coriander powder
- ½ tsp salt
- 1 cup semolina (rava/sooji) or breadcrumbs
- Oil for brushing

Method
- Wash the dals and soak them in water overnight. Rinse thoroughly and drain.
- Place the dals, garlic, ginger and green chillies in a blender and process to a coarse consistency. Transfer to a mixing bowl.
- Add the gram flour, coriander leaves, coriander powder, red chilli powder and salt. Mix well and allow to sweat till juices are drawn out.
- Press the mixture together to form lumps. If the mixture does not come together in lumps, add some more gram flour or breadcrumbs to bind it.
- Take small portions of the mixture and shape into croquettes or cutlets. Dredge with semolina or breadcrumbs if required.
- Put a frying pan on medium heat and brush with oil. When hot, place the croquettes or cutlets on the pan and cook, till well done on one side. Brush oil on the side facing up and gently flip each piece over. Cook, till well browned on the other side as well.
- Serve with a spicy chutney.

North Indian Daag Curry Base

I remember when I was newly married and had very little time in the kitchen, my sister-in-law taught me how to cook up a huge batch of this base gravy and keep it in the refrigerator. I would use it through the week to make quick curries, by simply heating oil, adding a few whole spices, stirring in a some spoonfuls of the base gravy and adding the main ingredient: meat, chicken, fish or vegetables.

Time: 1 hour | Makes: The base for 2 curries

Ingredients
- ¼ cup oil
- 1" piece of fresh ginger, finely chopped
- 4 garlic cloves, finely chopped
- 1-3 green chillies, minced
- 2 kg onions, diced fine
- ½ tbsp cumin powder
- 2 tsp coriander powder
- ¼ tsp turmeric powder
- ½ tsp garam masala powder
- 4 tomatoes, diced fine
- ½ tsp salt
- 3 tbsp chopped coriander leaves

Method
- Put the oil in a pan on low heat. When hot, add the ginger, garlic and green chillies. Stir-fry for 2-3 minutes. Ginger tends to burn and stick to the pan, so be vigilant.
- Add the onions and stir-fry, till dark brown but not burnt.
- Mix in the spice powders and continue to stir-fry for 1-2 minutes, till aromatic.
- Add the tomatoes, salt and coriander leaves and stir-fry for a minute longer.

- Cover the pan and cook, till the tomatoes are mixed in properly. The oil will separate from the dish at this point and rise to the surface.
- Remove from heat, cool, divide in half, transfer to airtight containers and freeze.

To use

- Defrost the curry base in one of the containers.
- Heat 1 tbsp of oil in a pan. Add 500 gms of vegetables, chicken or meat and the defrosted curry paste.
- Sauté for a few minutes, then add 1 cup of water and simmer, till your main ingredient is cooked and tender.

Mushroom Dum Biryani

Time: 1 hour | Serves: 4

Ingredients

Rice

- 1½ cups basmati rice
- 1 bay leaf
- 4 cloves
- 2 green cardamom pods
- 1 black cardamom pod
- 1" cinnamon stick
- 1 whole mace blade from 1 nutmeg
- ½ tsp cumin
- A pinch of salt

Mushrooms

- 1 tsp oil
- 2 onions, finely chopped
- 1" piece of fresh ginger, minced
- 5 garlic cloves, minced
- 2 tsp red chilli powder
- 1 tbsp coriander powder
- ½ tbsp black pepper powder
- ½ tsp turmeric powder
- ½ tbsp garam masala powder
- 2 tomatoes, puréed
- ⅛ cup coriander leaves
- ⅛ cup mint leaves
- ½ cup yoghurt, whisked smooth
- 1 tbsp milk
- 400 gms fresh mushrooms, rinsed and quartered
- ½ tbsp salt

To assemble the biryani
- ⅛ cup coriander leaves
- ⅛ cup mint leaves
- 1 tsp ghee
- 2 onions, finely sliced
- 10 saffron strands, soaked in ¼ cup of warm milk
- Sealing dough made with 2 cups wholewheat flour (atta) and ½ cup water

Method

Rice
- Wash the rice and soak it in water for 30 minutes.
- Bring about 3 cups of water to a boil in a large pan and add the whole spices and salt.
- Drain the rice and add it to the pan.
- Simmer on medium heat, till the rice is three-quarters cooked. Drain and reserve.

Mushrooms
- Put the oil in a pan on medium heat. When hot, add the chopped onions and sauté, till translucent.
- Add the ginger and garlic and sauté briefly.
- Sprinkle in the spice powders and stir-fry for a few seconds.
- Add the tomatoes and cook on high heat, till the masala is fairly thick.
- Wash the coriander leaves thoroughly in several changes of water. Drain well and chop fine.
- Add them to the pan along with the yoghurt and milk. Stir well and cook for about 2 minutes.
- Add the mushrooms and salt. Stir-fry on high heat for 2-3 minutes and then remove from heat.

To assemble the biryani
- Wash the leaves thoroughly in several changes of water. Drain well and chop fine.
- Put the ghee in a small pan on medium heat. Add the sliced onions and stir-fry, till crisp and brown.
- Layer the parboiled rice and mushroom masala in an ovenproof or microwave

dish that has a tight-fitting lid.
- Spread the fried onions on top.
- Sprinkle the soaked saffron milk and herbs over the onions.
- If baking in an oven, seal the lid on to the pan with the sealing dough and cook the biryani in an oven preheated to 200°C for 20 minutes.
- For the microwave, seal with plastic wrap and cook on medium for 15 minutes.

Sun-dried Tomato Pasta

Time: 20 minutes | Serves: 4

Ingredients

- ½ cup Italian extra virgin olive oil
- 12 garlic cloves, coarsely crushed
- 6 dried red chillies, broken
- 1 cup sun-dried tomatoes, julienned
- 1 cup coriander leaves or parsley
- 250 gms pasta (penne or fusilli)
- 1 cup vegetable stock
- Salt to taste

Method

- About 30 minutes before (or even the previous night) you plan to cook this dish, put the olive oil in a small deep pan on medium heat. When hot, add the garlic, red chillies and sun-dried tomatoes and cook for 1 minute.
- Switch off the heat and leave it for the flavours to develop. (The longer you leave it the better.)
- Wash the herbs thoroughly in several changes of water. Drain well and chop fine.
- When you're ready to assemble the dish, cook the pasta in plenty of boiling salted water, till al dente (page 150).
- Drain the pasta.
- Put a quarter of the pasta, a quarter of the flavoured oil and a quarter of the stock in a pan on medium heat. Toss well, till warmed through, add salt to taste and sprinkle with a quarter of the herbs.
- Transfer to plate and serve. Repeat with the rest of the pasta. Doing it in small batches allows the pasta to be evenly tossed and well coated in the flavoured oil.

Garlic Noodles / Pasta Alio Olio And Pasta Alio Olio E Pepperoncino

We once ate these noodles in a little hole-in-the-wall place near our house. It was delicious and I recreated it at home and it has stayed with us ever since. You can use just about any pasta but, my personal favourite are thin ones like capilleni or spaghetti No. 5, which are easy to eat. Here is a recipe for both a simple garlic pasta as well as a spicier option with chilli flakes.

The trick to getting this recipe right is to cook your pasta right.

Time: 30 minutes | Serves: 4

Ingredients
- 12 tsp sea salt
- 480 gms noodles or pasta
- ½ cup extra virgin olive oil
- ½ cup garlic cloves, smashed and finely chopped
- 1 cup chopped fresh parsley
- Salt and freshly ground black pepper to taste
- 2-3 tbsp chilli flakes (optional)

Method

To cook the pasta

- Cook the pasta in plenty of boiling, heavily salted water so it has room to 'swim' and doesn't end up clumping together.
- The ratio should be 1 litre of water per 100 grams of pasta (6 litres for 500 gms). If you don't use enough water the pasta will be gummy, so don't be kanjoos!
- Place the water to boil, add enough salt to make it as salty as seawater. (Get this right because you cannot correct it later.) Add 2-3 teaspoons of sea salt per litre. Neapolitans who are experts at cooking pasta, traditionally used sea

water to cook their pasta in times gone by.
- Once the water is boiling, add the pasta slowly so that it does not all land in the water at one time and reduce the temperature of the water. Keep adding a little pasta as the water returns to a boil.
- Don't break long pasta to fit the pan; use a wooden spoon to bend it as it cooks.
- Stir often and well to prevent it sticking to the bottom.
- Please, please do not add oil to your boiling water. No Italian cook adds oil to pasta water because that will not allow cooked pasta to absorb the sauce.
- Check on your pasta when it looks cooked. You can tell it's ready when it is al dente, or tender to the bite but with a slight resistance. The pasta package usually advises how long the pasta shape should be cooked, but don't trust it.
- A couple of minutes before it is supposed to be ready, fish out a piece and break it open; in the centre, you will see a white uncooked portion that called anima. If this is very big, continue cooking, till the anima is barely visible.
- At this point drain the pasta, giving it one or two good shakes to remove most of the water (it will continue to absorb water for a minute or two).
- Ladle a couple of spoons of the hot pasta water into a serving bowl, swirl it around to warm the bowl and pour it out.
- Transfer the cooked pasta to the bowl and reserve.

Sauce
- If you are quick, while the pasta is cooking, you can prepare the sauce. Aim to do this in small portions for best results.
- Put the oil in a heavy pan on medium heat. When hot, add the garlic and stir-fry, till it begins to turn pale gold. (Please, take the time to smell the cooking garlic and oil, it is the most beautiful aroma in the world.)
- If you would like to make alio olio e pepperoncino this is when you need to add the chilli flakes and stir-fry for about 30 seconds.
- Remove the pan from the heat and add ¾ of the parsley and salt and pepper to taste.
- Add the drained, still warm pasta and toss well, till all the pasta is coated. (If I'm not entertaining, I will often use the same pot as I cooked the pasta in so I have one less pot to clean.)
- Spoon on to warmed plates, garnish with the remaining parsley and serve immediately.

Root And Shoot Salad

About a year after we were married, we moved to Chandigarh. The idea was to explore the North, while also going closer to Dehra Dun and Shekhar's parents. On our first visit to Dehra Dun, after we settled down, I was touched to see that my father-in-law had planted an entire patch of lettuce in honour of my arrival because he knew I loved it! All that season we drove back from weekend trips with oodles of lettuce.

This salad was born out of one such trip when we returned with lettuce and turnips from our garden. The root vegetables and sprouts absorb all the fluid from the yoghurt, resulting in a crunchy cool, spicy mix. Great on its own or stuffed into rotis or pita.

Time: 10 minutes | Serves: 2-4

Ingredients

- ½ cup coriander leaves
- 1 cup mixed sprouts, steamed or cooked
- 1 potato, boiled and finely diced
- 1 carrot, finely diced and blanched
- 2 onions, finely chopped
- 1 turnip, finely diced
- 1 tsp finely chopped green chillies
- 2 cups yoghurt, whisked smooth
- Salt to taste
- A few lettuce leaves, shredded

Method

- Wash the coriander leaves thoroughly in several changes of water. Drain well and chop fine.

1. Rose and Pistachio Kehwa
2. Cutting Chai

1. Murrabba
2. A Gujarati Meal
3. Green Peppercorn Pickle

1. A Kutchi Meal
2. Nani's Date Cake
3. A Farsan Platter
4. Chundo
5. Rushina, her nani and her mother

4

1. Spice of Life
2. Cauliflower / Okra Tempura
3. Dal Soup
4. Dudhi nu Shaak

5

1. Ivy Gourd Moong Dal Salad
2. Spinach Soup
3. Phirni

6

1. Gujarati Dal Dhokli
2. Vatana na Ghugra
3. Mohanthal

7

1. Neha's Twist on Mayo Cake Chocolate Balls
2. 13-Onion Pasta
3. Mayo Chicken Curry

8

1. Neelu Bhabhi's Chole Bhature
2. Sun-dried Tomato Pasta
3. Railway Tomato Soup
4. Mushroom Dum Biryani

9

1. Pinky's Carrot Cake
2. Rainbow Idlis
3. Chocolate Hazelnut Spread
4. Broccoli and Cauliflower Pasta
5. Sesame Cauliflower

10

1. Natasha with a cookie baked by papa
2. Rose Pistachio Cake

11

1. Sheetal and her mother Usha
2. Ross' Momos
3. Usha's Maa ki Dal
4. Sindhi Curry

12

1. Cindy's Porridge or Congee
2. Hainanese Chicken Rice
3. Neha's Chilli Con Carne
4. Root Spinach Soup

13

1. Curry Leaf Fish
2. Rainbow Chard Sauté
3. Star Anise-scented Orange Chicken Pot Noodles

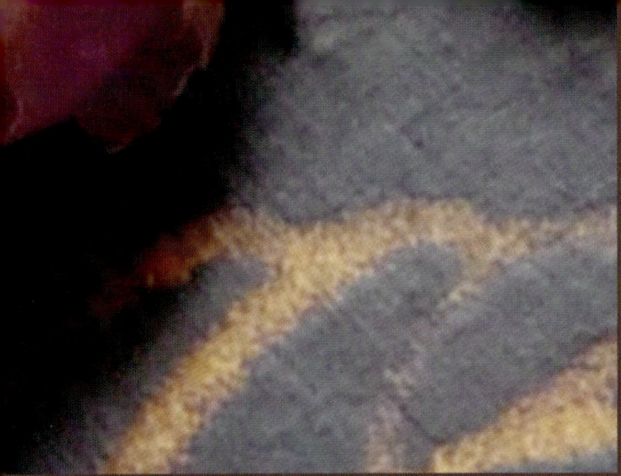

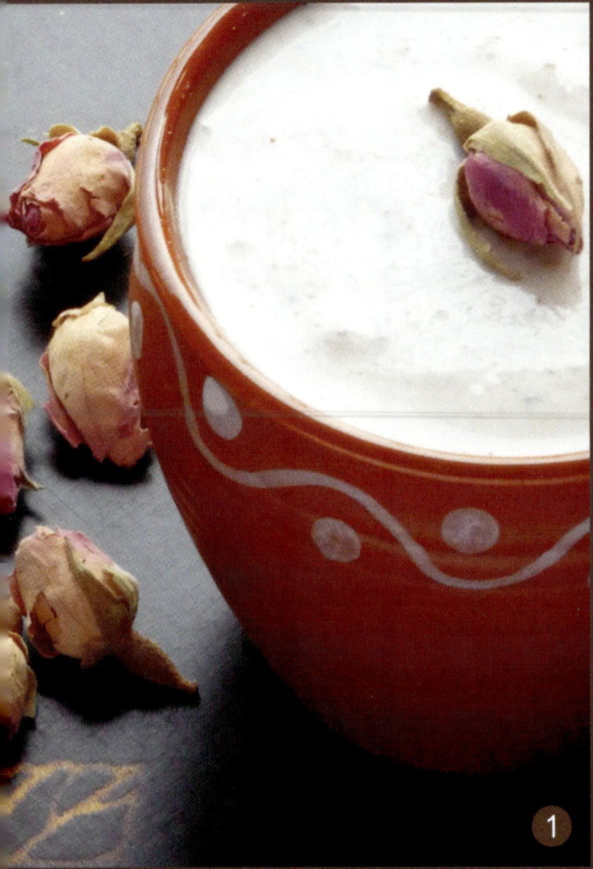

1

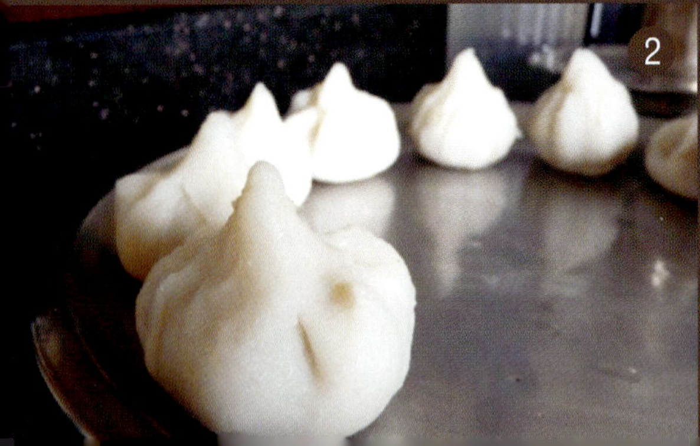

2

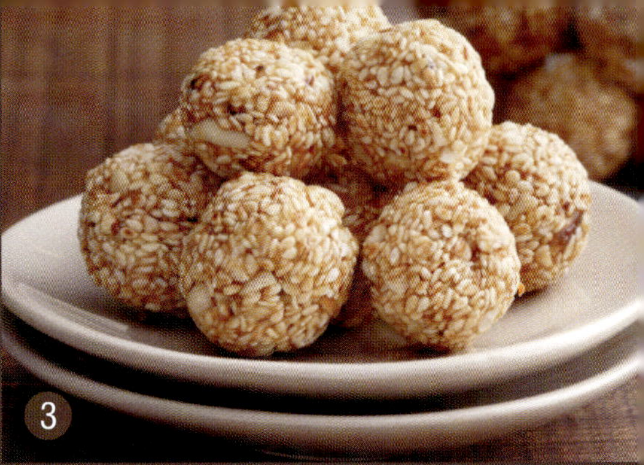

3

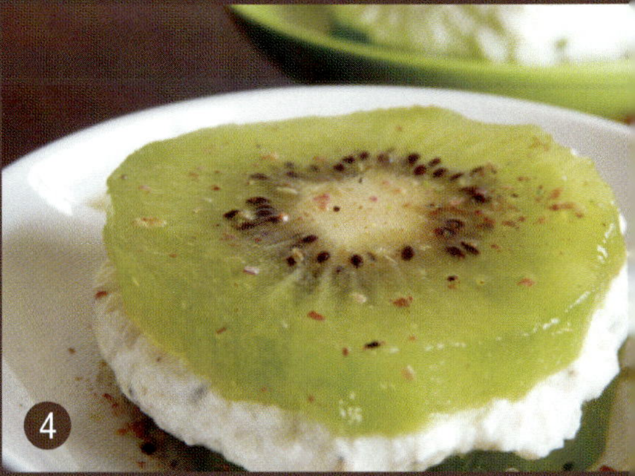

4

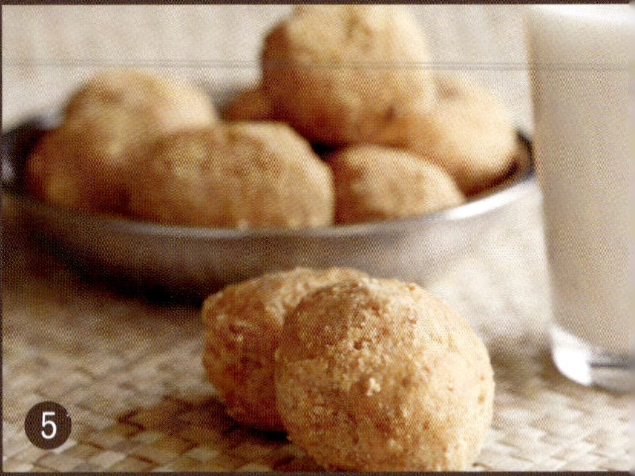

5

14

1. Lavender Pepper Vodka Thandai
2. Modak
3. Shobha's Tilache Laddu
4. Kiwi Fruit Sandesh
5. Maghas Laddu
6. Pomegranate Chocolate Mousse
7. Rose and Pistachio Labneh Balls

1. Aman and Natasha
2. Natasha loves nani's Diwali sweets
3. Rushina with her husband and children
4. Rushina

- Place them in a bowl with the sprouts, potato, carrot, onions, turnip, green chillies and yoghurt and mix well.
- Add salt to taste and leave it in the refrigerator, till ready to serve.
- Put a layer of shredded lettuce in a serving bowl and spoon the mixed salad over them.

Week's Worth Salad

I like having salads at every meal. In the initial days of marriage though, making lunch was not a priority. Still foggy from waking up, worried about getting out of the door with everything I needed and making it to that 8 a.m. train, I would never have time to cut salad on a daily basis. I resolved this by prepping a whole lot of ingredients (except tomatoes) on Sundays and refrigerating them in airtight containers. In the morning, I'd put together whatever veggies caught my fancy, and add a dressing.

Salad travels well and can give you variety from day to day. It's an easy routine; plus, if you get home late, you have lots of prepped ingredients to quickly make a meal.

Construction of my salad: I would begin with 2 parts assorted leafy greens and lettuce leaves (assorted lettuce and even Indian leafy greens such as spinach, mustard, chowli and fenugreek). Although it seems obvious to wash and portion out salads, if I did not have it ready and we were running late, it often deterred us from taking lunch. So I washed all the greens, hand tore them to keep browning to a minimum and spun them out to dry. Next, I put them into a container, with a paper towel at the bottom. (Condensation can form over the week and the paper towel absorbs things while keeping everything super fresh.)

To this I would add two parts of as many different vegetables as I liked. (This is of course a loose equation; seeing as most of us fall short in our daily intake of vegetables and since one really cannot get enough vegetables, this is one place I could pile them on.)

To make this salad a full meal I would add:

Any 3 servings of grain
- 1 slice bread (toasted/baked croutons)
- 1 cup ready-to-eat cereal (oats, muesli)
- ½ cup cereal
- ½ cup cooked rice or pasta
- 2 corn taco shells, broken up or
- 8 nachos chips
- 3 cups air-popped corn (or other seeds)

3-4 servings of vegetables
- 1 medium-sized potato, boiled
- ½ cup cooked or raw corn kernels
- 1 medium-sized tomato
- ½ cup raw or cooked vegetables

1-2 servings of fruit
- A melon wedge or 1 medium piece of any fruit
- ½ grapefruit
- ½ cup berries or grapes
- ¼ cup dried fruit

1 serving of dairy
- 1 cup yoghurt, whisked smooth
- 60 gms cheese, cubed
- ½ cup cubed paneer

1-2 servings of protein
- ⅓ cup cooked lean meat, poultry or fish
- ½ cup cooked beans
- 1 egg
- 2 tbsp peanut butter
- ⅓ cup nuts
- ½ cup tofu

Dressing

My formula for a vinaigrette is acidic ingredient + oil + salt + flavouring + optional sweetener

Once you have this formula in place, you can use it to get really creative. I start by blending my oil with pinches of any other flavourings and thoroughly combine them. Then drizzle in the acidic ingredient, blending with a whisk.

Acidic ingredients: The souring agent. You can use acidic fruit juices such as lime, orange, cranberry or even natural vinegars like red wine, white wine, champagne, apple cider, rice wine or balsamic vinegars.

Oil: The element that carries flavour, which is why it is very important in dressings. A little goes a long way. Experiment with extra virgin olive oils, exotic nut and seed oils and even flavoured ones.

Salt: You wouldn't think so, but the salt taste can be varied as well. Try sea salt, rock salt or salty condiments instead, such as soy sauce and Thai fish sauce, or even anchovies and salty cheeses.

Flavourings: The most obvious one is pepper of course, but you can also use other spices in combination with or instead of pepper. Other options include fresh and dried herbs, garlic, ginger and citrus zest.

Optional sweetener: The optional sweet ingredient is something I like to add to balance the other flavours. Try adding honey, sugar, sweet fruit juices, syrups.

Mushroom And Potato Gratin

Time: 1 hour | Serves: 4-6

Ingredients
- 400 gms potatoes
- 3 tbsp olive oil
- 1 bay leaf
- 200 gms mushrooms, sliced thick
- Butter for greasing
- 200 ml double cream
- 100 ml milk
- 10 garlic cloves, chopped
- ½ tsp salt
- 50 gms grated Cheddar cheese

Method
- Boil the potatoes in salted water, till cooked but firm. Peel and cut into thick slices.
- Put the olive oil in a pan on medium heat. When hot, add the bay leaf.
- Add the mushrooms in small batches and stir-fry, till all the moisture has bubbled off and they are crisp and golden at the edges.
- Layer the potatoes in a buttered baking dish with the mushrooms.
- Combine the cream, milk, garlic and salt in a bowl and pour it over the layered potatoes and mushrooms.
- Sprinkle the cheese on top and bake in an oven preheated to 180°C for 30-40 minutes, till the top is golden.

Green Garlic And Coriander Frittata With Tomato Chutney

This omelette is inspired by the classic herb omelette. The slow cooking infuses the omelette with the aroma of the green garlic, and the garlic bits in contact with the pan get deliciously crisp and crunchy. The pairing with the tomato chutney that keeps the omelette getting too eggy or garlicky happened much later. I picked up the recipe from Mrs Kirti Madhok, the mother of my sister's best friend Aditi Madhok. I had an opportunity to stay with them for one idyllic weekend during a Rajasthani winter and this chutney was on the menu for breakfast one day. Steaming hot and fragrant with ginger, it will always remind me of Kirti Aunty, whose cooking I hope to get more of someday.

Time: 20 minutes | Serves: 1

Ingredients

Frittata

- ¼ cup finely chopped green garlic
- ¼ cup finely chopped coriander leaves
- 1 tbsp finely chopped green chillies
- 2 eggs or 2 or 3 egg whites, beaten with a pinch of salt
- 1-2 tbsp oil

Tomato chutney

- 1 tsp oil
- 2-3 slices of green chilli (optional)
- 2 medium-sized tomatoes, grated
- 1" piece of fresh ginger, grated
- A pinch of sugar
- Salt to taste

Method

Frittata

- Combine the green garlic, coriander leaves and green chillies in a bowl and mix well. Add the eggs and mix well again.
- Put the oil in a frying pan on medium heat. (Use a small pan if you are using 2 egg whites only, or the omelette will be too thin and crisp.)
- When the oil is hot, and add the egg mixture.
- Reduce the heat to the lowest and cook, till set.
- Top with tomato chutney and serve.

Tomato chutney

- While the omelette is on the pan, place another pan on medium heat.
- Pour in the oil and when hot, add the green chilli and allow it to crackle.
- Add the tomatoes and cook, till the liquid is released.
- Let the liquid evaporate and add the ginger, sugar and salt.
- Simmer, till the ginger is cooked and its aroma is released.

Keema Lasagne

When I decided to cook a special birthday dinner for my nephew, Rohan, just before I left for Kerala, I ambitiously but rather worriedly planned lasagne. It had been a full day at work — reviewing a restaurant at lunch, followed by a couple of meetings before I could get home to work. Lasagne from scratch is an epic recipe. I made it entirely out of my head, based on tasting it once at a little café in Italy a few weeks after I was married. With no pasta machine, it took me two days to get the whole thing done, using a rolling pin to make the pasta, slow-cooking the sauce, but it was worth it, because Shekhar still sings its praises! Home-made pasta sheets layered with a spicy keema-style sauce and cheese. The great thing about this dish is you can make larger batches of the keema and pasta sheets ahead of time and freeze in individual portions. When you are ready to eat, just assemble and bake.

Time: 1 hour | Serves: 4

Ingredients

Pasta sheets (for 4-5 sheets; you can also use ready-made pasta sheets)

- 250 gms refined flour (maida)
- ½ tsp freshly ground black pepper
- 2 tbsp olive oil
- 2 eggs, whisked

Keema

- ⅓ cup oil
- 1 tsp sugar
- 2 black cardamom pods
- 4 green cardamom pods,
- 1" cinnamon stick

- 4-5 cloves
- ½ tsp whole black peppercorns
- 1 bay leaf
- 1 tsp freshly ground black pepper
- 2 tbsp finely sliced green chillies
- 1 cup finely chopped garlic
- 2 cups finely chopped onions
- 1 tsp grated fresh ginger
- 500 gms chicken, minced
- 4 cups tomato purée
- 1 tsp garam masala powder
- 2 tsp butter
- ½ cup finely chopped coriander leaves
- Salt to taste

To assemble
- 1 large or 2 small baking dishes
- 250 gms Mozzarella cheese, grated

Method

Pasta sheets
- Sift the flour and pepper into a bowl.
- Add the oil and rub with your fingertips, till it resembles breadcrumbs.
- Add the eggs and knead them in as well as possible.
- Slowly add cold water, a little at a time, kneading well to form a smooth dough.
- Divide into 5 portions and roll out as thin as possible. Trim each portion to the shape and size of your container and lay out to dry for about 10 minutes.
- To store, bake on a tava or griddle on medium heat on both sides for a couple of minutes or till small brown dots appear.
- Cool and roll the sheets, separated by foil, and freeze.

Keema
- Put the oil in a large pan on medium heat. When hot, add the sugar and cook, till dissolved. (This will help caramelise the onions quicker.)
- Add the whole spices and sauté, till they are a shade darker and aromatic.

- Add the ground black pepper and green chillies and sauté for a few seconds, ensuring that neither burns.
- Add one-third of the garlic and sauté, till slightly brown at the edges.
- Add all the onions and sauté, till well browned.
- Mix in the ginger and sauté for 1 minute.
- Add the mince, salt and remaining garlic. Stir well, cover and cook, till the mince loses all its juices. Open and cook, till dry and well browned.
- Pour in the tomato purée, cover and cook, till the oil rises to the surface.
- Stir in the garam masala powder and simmer, till slightly (but not completely) dried out. Add the butter and coriander leaves and mix well.
- Add salt to taste. Mix again and set aside to cool.

To assemble

- Spread a little keema on the base of the baking dish. Lay a pasta sheet on top.
- Spoon and spread a little keema over the pasta sheet.
- Scatter grated cheese.
- Repeat layering, till all the ingredients are used, saving the thinnest pasta sheet for the top.
- Scatter with cheese and cover the dish with foil.
- Bake in an oven preheated to 180°C for 35-40 minutes.
- Remove the foil and bake uncovered for about 10 minutes, till the cheese is golden brown.
- Serve hot.

Cabbage Yoghurt Salad

I concocted this recipe one night, using whatever I had in a rather bare refrigerator.

Time: 20 minutes | Serves: 4

Ingredients
- 250 gms (1 head) cabbage, cut into thin strips
- 1 tbsp sesame oil
- 10 dried red, round, boria chillies
- 1 cup yoghurt, whisked smooth
- ½ cup halved and sliced tomatoes
- Salt to taste

Method
- Blanch the cabbage in 5 cups of boiling salted water for 4-5 minutes, till it softens and brightens in colour slightly.
- Drain and squeeze tightly using your hands, depositing the squeezed cabbage in a mixing bowl as you go along. Set aside.
- Put the oil in a small pan on medium heat. When hot, add the red chillies. Stir-fry, till they begin to scorch. Your oil should be a lovely tint of red by now.
- Switch off the heat and add the yoghurt. Mix well and pour the contents of the pan over the cabbage.
- Add the tomatoes and mix thoroughly.
- Taste, add more salt if required and serve.

My Le Crueset Bean Cassoulet

It was quite a while since I jumped up and down in excitement over something. But when I received my thirty-fifth birthday gift from Shekhar — a piece of Le Crueset cookware — I did! I cannot tell you how many times I have sighed over this lovely enamel cookware, caressed it lovingly and walked away! I had a pile of work to do the day it arrived but it wasn't every day that one acquired a Le Crueset and I just HAD to cook something that night. I set it on the desk near me and kept wandering off mentally, ruminating over what to cook. Finally I compromised on a spiced up bean cassoulet because my vegetarian mother was coming to dinner.

Time: 1 hour | Serves: 4-6

Ingredients

- ¼ cup olive oil
- 3 medium-sized onions, finely chopped
- 2 medium-sized carrots, finely chopped
- 3 green bell peppers, finely chopped
- 1 tbsp chopped garlic
- 2 tbsp minced green chillies
- 1 bay leaf
- 1 star anise flowers (badian)
- 1" cinnamon stick
- 4 cloves
- ½ tsp whole black peppercorns
- 2 cans (400 gms drained weight) cannellini beans
- 2 tbsp dried oregano

Method

- Put the oil in a pan on medium heat. When hot, add the onions, carrots, bell

peppers, garlic, green chillies, bay leaf and whole spices. Cook on medium to low heat for about 15 minutes, stirring occasionally, till the vegetables are soft, golden and aromatic.
- Stir in the beans.
- Pour in 5 cups of water and mix in the oregano. Simmer, partially covered, stirring occasionally, till everything is cooked and has a delicious aroma.
- Serve in large bowls with crusty bread and a green salad on the side.

Pasta From Scratch With White Wine Sauce

Time: 45 minutes + 1 hour for dough to rest | Serves: 4-6

Ingredients

Pasta dough

- 1½ cups refined flour (maida) + extra for rolling
- ¼ cup semolina (rava/sooji)
- 1 tsp salt
- 2 large or 3 medium-sized eggs
- 1 tsp olive oil

White wine sauce

- 1 tbsp unsalted butter
- 1 tbsp olive oil
- 2 onions, chopped
- 1 garlic clove, finely chopped
- ⅓ cup dry white wine
- ½ cup chicken stock
- 2 tbsp cream
- Salt and freshly ground black pepper to taste

Method

Pasta dough

- Combine the semolina, flour and the salt in a large mixing bowl. Make a well in the centre of the bowl.
- Crack the eggs into the well and pour in the olive oil.
- Mix the flour into the liquid with a fork, using a gentle swirling motion that starts at the centre of the bowl and slowly moves outwards. Keep mixing and drawing in larger quantities of flour, till all the flour has been mixed.
- When the dough starts resisting the fork, use your hands to bring the dough together into a ball.
- Dust with flour if the dough is too wet and difficult to manage. Add more

water (slowly) if the dough feels too dry. If your semolina is coarse, the dough will feel grainy in your hands. Don't worry. It'll soften after resting.
- Now, knead this ball of dough for 8-10 minutes. Remember, the more you knead, the better its texture will be. Use the ball of your hand (palm open) to flatten the dough. Fold the flattened dough and repeat the process.
- Once the dough is ready (poke a finger into it; it should return into shape), form it into a ball and return it to the bowl. Cover and let it rest for around 1 hour at room temperature.
- Your pasta dough is ready!
- You can make hand-made pasta by rolling the dough into thin chapattis, and then cutting into ½-cm strips. You can also use the rolled sheets to make lasagne. You can roll them into small discs which can be then stuffed to make ravioli.
- If you have a pasta machine, follow the instructions provided by the manufacturer for rolling out the dough. For this pasta recipe, I recommend you roll the dough down to a minimum setting of 2, after which the pasta is likely to tear.

White wine sauce
- Melt the butter along with the olive oil in a large frying pan on medium heat. Add the onions and garlic and cook, till softened.
- Stir in the wine and cook, till heated through.
- Pour in the stock and continue cooking for about 5 minutes, till the sauce is reduced and slightly thickened.
- Add the cream and stir well.
- Mix in salt and pepper to taste.
- Serve the sauce over the cooked pasta.

Rose And Pistachio Cake

Time: 1 hour 20 minutes | Serves: 6-8

Ingredients

Cake

- 1 ⅓ cup rose sugar (see note on page 169)
- ½ cup butter
- 2 eggs
- 2 tsp vanilla extract
- 1½ cups refined flour (maida)
- 1¾ tsp baking powder
- ½ cup milk
- 2 tbsp marmalade

Butter cream frosting (Time: 10 minutes; Makes: about 3 cups of icing)

- 2 cups butter
- 1 tbsp vanilla extract
- 4 cups sifted icing sugar
- 2 tbsp lime juice

Garnish

- 2 cups powdered pistachio
- 1 cup rosebuds/petals

Method

Cake

- Grease and lightly flour a 9"x 9" pan or line a muffin pan with paper liners.
- Cream the sugar and butter together in a bowl, till light and fluffy.
- Beat in the eggs, one at a time. Beat well between each addition, till well incorporated before adding the next.
- Stir in the vanilla.
- Sift the flour and baking powder into another bowl.

- Fold it gently into the creamed mixture.
- Finally stir in milk, a little at a time, till the batter is smooth.
- Spoon the batter into the prepared pan.
- Put it into and oven preheated to 175°C and bake the cake for 30-40 minutes; or the cupcakes for 20-25 minutes. The cake is cooked when it springs back to the touch.
- Turn out on to a wire rack and set aside, till cool.

Butter cream frosting
- Cream the butter in large bowl with an electric mixer.
- Add the vanilla.
- Gradually add the sugar, a cup at a time, beating well on medium speed, till it is well incorporated. Scrape down the sides and bottom of the bowl often.
- When all sugar has been mixed in, the icing will appear dry.
- Add the lime juice and beat at medium speed, till light and fluffy.
- Keep the bowl covered with a damp cloth, till ready to use.
- For best results, keep it in the refrigerator when not in use. Refrigerated in an airtight container, this icing can be stored for up to 2 weeks.
- Rewhip before using.

To decorate
- Frost the cake, sprinkle with powdered pistachios and decorate with rosebuds or petals.

Note: *To make rose sugar, crush equal volumes of sugar and dried rose petals together.*

Clove-scented Lamb In Red Wine

Time: 1 hour + 1 hour for marination | Serves: 4-6

Ingredients

Marinade

- 1 tsp salt
- ⅔ tsp freshly ground black pepper
- 1½ tbsp cloves
- 3 black cardamom pods
- 8 garlic cloves, crushed

Lamb

- 500 gms lamb, fat trimmed
- 3 tbsp olive oil
- 1 tbsp chopped onion
- 1 tbsp chopped carrot
- 1 tbsp chopped celery
- 2 tbsp refined flour (maida)
- 200 gms onions, quartered
- 200 gms baby potatoes, peeled and kept whole
- 2 cups chicken stock
- 1½ cup Dindori Reserve Shiraz

Garnish

- 2 tbsp chopped parsley

Method

- Combine the marinade ingredients in a bowl.
- Wash the meat, pat dry and cut it into 1" cubes.
- Mix the marinade into the meat and leave for 1 hour.
- Put a skillet on medium heat. When hot, add the oil and the meat.
- Stir-fry, till the meat is well browned and beginning to crisp at the edges.

- Remove from the pan and reserve.
- Add the chopped onion, carrot and celery to the pan and stir-fry for a minute.
- Stir in the flour and cook, till it is well blended.
- Add the quartered onions and whole baby potatoes and stir-fry, till the potatoes are almost cooked.
- Add the partially cooked lamb and stir-fry, till almost cooked through.
- Pour in the stock and wine and mix well. Taste and add more salt and pepper, if required.
- Mix well and simmer, till the meat and potatoes are tender.
- Garnish with chopped parsley and serve.

Roasted Pumpkin Soup With Spiced Cointreau Butter And Candied Orange Zest

Time: 1 hour | Serves: 2-4

Ingredients

Cointreau butter

- 250 gms butter, softened
- ¾ cup castor sugar
- 1 tsp finely grated orange rind
- ¼ cup Cointreau

Candied orange zest

- 3 thick-skinned oranges
- 1 cup sugar
- 1 tbsp honey
- ½ cup Cointreau

Soup

- 250 gms red pumpkin, diced
- ½ cup diced carrots
- 1 litre vegetable stock or water
- 2 tbsp oil
- 1" piece of fresh ginger, finely chopped
- ½ tsp garam masala powder
- Salt to taste

Method

Cointreau butter

- Beat the butter with a wooden spoon or electric beater for about 10 minutes, till light and fluffy.
- Add the sugar and continue to beat, till well incorporated and almost dissolved. (You can use icing sugar if you prefer a completely smooth butter, although the crunch is appreciated by many.)

- Gradually add the Cointreau, beating between additions, till well combined.
- Spread the butter on a piece of foil. Take one edge of the foil and roll the butter over to shape into a cylinder.
- Mark the roll lightly to divide and freeze, till solid.

Candied orange zest
- Wash the oranges well and pat dry.
- Using a zesting tool, remove the orange part of the rind in long, thin strips starting at the top of the orange and with even pressure continue all the way to the bottom. Continue removing all the zest in strips.
- Place the zest in a heavy pan of boiling water. Reduce the heat to a simmer and cook for 5 minutes.
- Drain and rinse with cold water.
- Add the sugar, honey and 1 cup of water to the same pan in which the zest was cooked.
- Bring to a boil on high heat, stirring continuously. Stop stirring when it comes to a boil.
- Add the drained and rinsed zest and cover with a tight-fitting lid. Reduce the heat to low and cook for about 15 minutes without disturbing it.
- Remove from heat and allow to cool in the covered pan.
- Add the Cointreau and refrigerate the candied orange in the syrup in an airtight container. Store for up to a month.

Soup
- Cook the diced pumpkin and carrot in the oven or on a pan, till well browned.
- Cool and purée them in a blender with a little stock or water and set aside.
- Put the oil in a large, deep pan on medium heat. When hot, add the ginger and garam masala powder.
- Add the puréed pumpkin and carrot and stir well.
- Pour in the remaining stock and bring to a boil, stirring well.

To serve
- Spoon the soup into warm soup bowls.
- Slice the Cointreau butter into discs and arrange them on a plate to be served on the side, or drop a slice into each bowl.
- Serve the soup with crostini on the side, spread with any pâté and sprinkled with the candied orange zest.

Bourbon And Rosemary Mutton Potato Pie

Time: 1 hour + overnight for marination | Serves: 6

Ingredients

Marinade

- 2 sprigs fresh rosemary
- 1 tbsp ginger-garlic paste
- ¾ cup bourbon
- 1 tsp salt

Mutton

- 1 kg boneless mutton
- 1 tbsp butter
- 1 tsp freshly ground black pepper
- ¾ tsp chilli flakes
- 1-2 sprigs of fresh rosemary
- 250 gms onions, cut in chunks
- 8 garlic cloves, crushed
- 1 cup mutton stock
- ⅓ cup Jack Daniels BBQ sauce
- ½ cup bourbon
- 2 tbsp refined flour (maida)

Potatoes

- 2 tbsp oil
- 6 garlic cloves, chopped
- 3-4 sprigs of fresh rosemary
- ½ cup milk
- 800 gms potatoes
- 1 tbsp butter
- 1 tsp salt

Method

Mutton

- Combine the marinade ingredients in a large bowl.
- Wash the meat, pat dry and cut into 1" cubes.
- Add the meat to the marinade and mix well with your hands, ensuring that it is well covered in the marinade. Leave overnight in the refrigerator.
- Melt the butter in a pan on low to medium heat. Add the black pepper, chilli flakes and rosemary and fry for 30-40 seconds.
- Add the onions and garlic and fry for 1-2 minutes.
- Mix in the marinated meat and fry, till well browned. Remove from heat.
- Stir in the flour.
- Combine the stock, BBQ sauce and bourbon and pour it in gradually, stirring after each addition, till well combined.
- Return the pan to heat and cook for a further 5 minutes, stirring continuously, till the sauce is thick.
- Remove from heat and reserve.

Potatoes

- Put the oil in a pan on medium heat. When hot, add the garlic and fry, till well browned and crisp. Add the rosemary and cook, till it darkens slightly in colour.
- Remove from heat and crush the contents of the pan lightly.
- Heat the milk, till hot but not boiling and add the crushed garlic and rosemary. Leave to infuse.
- Put the potatoes into a pan of boiling salted water and cook for 20 minutes, till tender. Drain and when cool enough to handle, peel them.
- Return the potatoes to the pan and add the butter, infused milk and salt.
- Mash, till smooth. Reserve.

To cook the pie

- Spoon the meat into an ovenproof dish and top with the mashed potato.
- Bake in an oven preheated to 180°C for 15 minutes, till golden on top.
- Serve with a good bread.

Yummy Mummy
aka Chief Cook, Espionage Agent

The first two years are a breeze: breast-feeding is extremely convenient because carrying sustenance as a mother does, makes feeding and keeping kids full, easy. The move to solid food is still manageable because the kids do not know they have a choice. Till then you serve meals in the belief that they will be consumed. Spinach is spinach and beetroot is beetroot and your child has to eat it, because you tell him he doesn't have a choice. Then comes the day he will say, 'I do have a choice!' Yep, can't argue with that!

Planning meals is a steep upward climb of the food pyramid. I mean how does one serve 'something nice' at every meal? And then comes school! With great fanfare you welcome the tiffin/lunch box phase of motherhood. If there is anything that will make you appreciate your mother a thousand-fold, it is this phase. Every morning brings the challenge of 'What to pack for lunch?' Just so your kids will like it enough to eat! And every evening brings a discussion of 'His-dabba-is-better-than-mine … he got Maggi! Mine is so boring! Why can't you give me nice dabbas?' I found my inspiration from Calvin's (of the comic book fame) long-suffering mother. She discovered the FMCG mantra to package things the way your customers want to see them and who am I to argue? I plated up 'Worms in Monster Blood' for dinner, ignoring Shekhar's gagging and rolling eyeballs and waited, with bated breath, for a reaction from the third person at the table. There was none, unless you count furious slurping as a reaction. E-V-E-R-Y to S to T to R to A to N to D of my gorily rechristened spaghetti in spinach sauce went down his gullet! And he asked for more! I began to routinely sneak Monster Blood (spinach purée) into everything and served Dragon Flesh (beetroot salad), Monkey Brains (paneer bhurji) or other revolting but innovatively named stomach-churning dishes regularly. If your hackles aren't raised yet, try Ant Soup (dal with mustard tadka)! I also discovered and used cookie cutters with a vengeance, creating food pictures of vegetables and roti, fish and starfish swimming through spinach seaweed on blue plates. My Star and Moon Idli platters and Broccoli Tree Forests complete with vegetable animals were masterpieces!

But seriously, ultimately, being a mother is not all that difficult. I should know, because when Aman was a little over five years, I chose to give it another shot. And learned that every pregnancy and every child is different. Natasha is the total antithesis of her brother who is an angel even at his worst.

With her, I have sunk to lower depths. I've mastered the art of disguise (ing food)! Sharpened up my arsenal with anything that has the ability to render detested vegetables to a size that can sneak into the tiniest pasta crevice or cling inseparably to rice so they can't be picked out. And I smuggle, SMUGGLE these vegetables into everything!

But my miniature tornado just will not eat her vegetables! Mercifully she eats fruit and raw carrot and cucumber so I still hope.

I also have a trick up my sleeve! Cooking with her! When Aman grew older, I began cooking with him. It taught Aman about nutrition and healthy eating in a very defining way that no amount of nagging would have achieved. But cooking has also instilled eating habits I hope will last him a lifetime, to a love for fruit and vegetables for instance! And hopefully he will also remember the more important things later, like balanced diets and the importance of wholegrain. I am also hopeful it is creating memories that they, in turn, can pass on to their children one day.

Natasha already rolls rotis (one problem she will never face like her mother did) and wants to see and smell everything in the kitchen, often saying 'main badi ho ke aapki tarah Yummy Mummy banoongi'. Whether the same will happen with Natasha I suspect will have to wait for a future book.

Chicken Mexican Wrap

This is a healthier version of the wrap served by a popular international burger chain in India. I discovered that the trick to get the flavour right is in the combination of celery and chilli garlic sauce. You can shape the patties into long ovals for wraps and round discs for burgers.

Time: 25 minutes | Serves: 4

Ingredients

Chicken Patties

- 350-400 gms boneless, skinned chicken breasts
- 2 tbsp cold chicken stock
- 2 tbsp fine oatmeal or cornstarch
- 1 tsp salt
- ½ tsp freshly ground black pepper
- 2 egg whites
- 3 cups oil for deep-frying, or as needed
- Oatmeal or refined flour (maida) for dredging

Salad

- ¼ cup shredded red cabbage
- ¼ cup shredded white cabbage
- ¼ cup grated carrot
- ¼ cup lettuce leaves, torn to bite-sized bits
- 2 tbsp finely sliced celery

Wraps

- 4 large rotis 12" in diameter or more (I make these with wholewheat or multigrain flour)
- 4 processed Cheddar cheese slices
- 4 tbsp home-made mayonnaise (page 127)

- 4 tsp Sriracha chilli sauce or other (Sriracha is a Chinese sauce that gives a distinct flavour to this dish)

Method

Chicken patties

- Cut the chicken breasts into bite-sized chunks and place in a food processor. Set at low speed and mince.
- Add the stock, a few drops at a time, and continue to blend slowly, till you have a paste-like consistency.
- Add the oatmeal or cornstarch, salt and pepper, blend lightly to combine well and transfer to a bowl.
- Beat the egg whites, till they are just beginning to stiffen and carefully fold into the chicken mixture.
- Put the oil for deep-frying in a kadhai or wok on medium heat, till really hot.
- Shape the chicken mixture into patties, dredge with oatmeal or flour and drop them into the hot oil.
- Fry for 1-1½ minutes, turn over and fry the other side for the same time.
- Remove and drain on kitchen paper.

Salad

- Combine all the vegetables in a bowl. Mix well and set aside.

To assemble the wraps

- Position a roti on your workspace in front of you. Place a patty in the middle. Top with a strip of cheese, mayonnaise, chilli sauce and salad.
- Fold the bottom flap over the edge of your patty. Be generous with the amount of roti you fold over; it will be the only barrier between the filling and the diner's lap!
- Now fold the left side over the filling, tucking the edge of the roti under the filling on the opposite side.
- Fold the right side over the left. This is the key to holding the whole wrap together and maintaining its integrity. Bring the top flap over the bottom.
- Serve warm.

Spaghetti in Spinach Sauce
(Worms in Monster Blood for Some!)

Time: 25 minutes | Serves: 3-4

Ingredients
- 1 kg spinach
- 1 tbsp butter
- 1 cup sliced onions
- 4 garlic cloves, minced
- A little water or stock for thinning
- 250 gms spaghetti

To serve
- ½ cup freshly grated Parmesan cheese

Method
- Clean and wash the spinach thoroughly in several changes of water.
- Drain and blanch it in boiling water for 1 minute, till it wilts and darkens to a bright green. Drain, squeeze dry and chop it coarsely.
- Put the butter in a pan on medium heat. When hot, add the onion. Sauté, till translucent.
- Add the garlic and sauté for 1 minute.
- Mix in the spinach and stir-fry, till bright green. Remove from heat and cool.
- Cook the spaghetti in plenty of boiling salted water, till al dente (page 150).
- When the spinach stir-fry is cool, blend it to a paste using a little water or stock, if required, to thin it down.
- Reheat it gently and add the cooked spaghetti.
- Stir properly so that the spaghetti is well coated.
- Serve warm with grated Parmesan on the side.

Sesame Potato Footballs

'These are very yummy and I like them because I do,' is what Aman has to say about them. As articulate as he is, it really is amazing how much he does love them. The potatoes work as a fuel in the form of simple carbs, while the spinach and sesame add texture.

Time: 10 minutes | Serves: 2

Ingredients
- ½ cup spinach leaves
- ½ cup toasted white sesame seeds (til)
- 2 tbsp black sesame seeds (til)
- 1 cup boiled and mashed potatoes
- 2 tbsp cream cheese
- Salt to taste
- Pepper to taste

Method
- Clean and wash the spinach thoroughly in several changes of water. Drain and shred it.
- Combine the two types of sesame seeds and spread them on a plate.
- Mix the mashed potato, spinach, cream cheese, salt and pepper in a bowl.
- Taste and adjust the salt and pepper.
- Shape into smooth walnut-sized balls and roll in the sesame seed mix.
- Arrange the balls in a tiffin box.
- Stick a patch of net to one side of the tiffin box to really get into things!

Chocolate Hazelnut Spread

Chocolate sauce or spread is a favourite around our home, but much as I love it, its nutritional qualities are nothing to write home about. Store-bought versions are very high in sugar and added fat. I decided to make my own. Not only was it easy, but I could control the sugar content which I felt allowed the flavour of the nuts to come into their own. Also, all the fat in it comes from the nuts, like a chocolate-flavoured nut butter. While nuts are high in fat, they are high in the fat we are advised to eat.

Time: 40 minutes | Makes: 300 gms of chocolate spread

Ingredients
- 1 cup sugar
- 1 vanilla pod
- 2 cups whole raw hazelnuts
- ¼ cup unsweetened dark cocoa powder

Method
- Place the sugar and the vanilla pod in a coffee grinder and powder.
- Sift it through a sieve into a bowl. Grind any remaining large bits again and repeat. Reserve.
- Put a dry kadhai or wok on medium heat. When hot, roast the hazelnuts for about 10 minutes, till you get the aroma of roasted nuts and they darken slightly. Set aside to cool.
- (If you are using hazelnuts with skins, you will have to peel them. To do this, place cooled hazelnuts between two sheets of newspaper and rub, till most of the skin comes off.)
- Place the prepared nuts in a blender and process. As their oils are extracted, they tighten up into a mass that looks like it will break your blender. Keep your blender going though, and soon you will see, almost like magic, that they will become liquid (about 7 minutes).

- Add the cocoa powder and half the powdered sugar mix and continue to blend, till well combined.
- Taste for sweetness and add sugar if required. (Any leftover sugar can be used in other dishes; the vanilla adds a lovely flavour to anything — even coffee).
- Once you have achieved the sweetness you want, transfer your chocolate spread to an airtight jar and store in the refrigerator for up to 2 months.
- Stir before using and spread on anything from bread to cakes and even rotis!

Fruit Pizza

Time: 20 minutes | Makes: 1 large cake or 16 pieces

Ingredients
- 1 cup thick, hung yoghurt, whisked smooth
- 4 tsp honey
- 250 gm bar sponge cake or sweet wholemeal bread, sliced into ¾" thick slices
- 250 gms assorted fresh fruit, finely sliced (strawberries, blueberries, raspberries, kiwi fruit, oranges)

Garnish
- 1 cup almonds, skinned, toasted and flaked

Method
- Put the hung yoghurt in a small bowl. Stir in half the honey, mix well and chill, till required.
- Spread the yoghurt mixture evenly over the sliced cake or bread and arrange the fruit attractively on top. Drizzle the extra honey on top if you like.
- Sprinkle with toasted almond flakes.
- You could cover with a slice of bread to make a fruit sandwich for easy packing.

Trail Mix Treasures

Trail mix is a great snack because it includes a variety of foods that provide fibre, protein and sugar to satisfy all kinds of cravings. I like to use these 'sweets' as rewards rather than commercial candy and chocolate bars.

Time: 10 minutes | Makes: 40 pieces

Ingredients
- ½ cup shelled pumpkin seeds
- ½ cup peanuts, crushed
- ½ cup walnuts, crushed
- ½ cup cashewnuts, crushed
- ½ cup almonds, crushed
- 1 cup seedless raisins
- 1 cup dried fruit
- ¼ cup dried coconut slivers

Method
- Combine all the ingredients in a bowl and mix well.
- Spoon into small pouches or wrap with cellophane into candy shapes.
- Stick a patch of net to one side of the tiffin box to really get into things!

Broccoli And Cauliflower Pasta

Time: 1¼ hours | Serves: 4-6

Ingredients
- ½ cup almond flakes
- 1 packet (250 gms) tri-coloured pasta
- 1 tbsp + 1 tbsp olive oil
- 1 cup cauliflower florets
- Salt to taste
- 1 cup broccoli florets
- 2 medium-sized onions, sliced ¼" wide lengthwise
- 4 garlic cloves, finely chopped
- 1 tbsp Italian herb blend
- 2 tbsp seedless golden raisins, soaked in warm water for 30 minutes and drained
- 2 tbsp dried sour cherries
- 2 tbsp chopped parsley

To serve
- 1 tbsp chopped parsley
- 4 tbsp grated Parmesan cheese

Method
- Lightly toast the almond flakes and set aside.
- Cook the pasta according to package directions, till al dente (or see page 150). Drain, reserving 1 cup of the water. Reserve the pasta and the water.
- Place a large, heavy, non-stick pan on medium heat. When hot, add 1 tbsp of oil.
- Add the cauliflower. Raise the heat to high and add a generous amount of salt (the vegetables should be seasoned right from the start, otherwise they will be bland; taste to check halfway through cooking).
- Stir-fry the cauliflower, till it is tender and starting to get golden in spots.

- Add the broccoli at this point and sauté. Cook the vegetables, till they are both well browned in spots. Remove the vegetables from the pan and reserve.
- Using the same pan (rinse if needed), add 1 tbsp of oil and sauté the onions on medium heat, till they begin to soften.
- Add the garlic, herb blend and a pinch of salt. Be careful not to let the garlic burn. Cook, till the onions are translucent.
- Put another pan on very low heat. Add the pasta cooking water and the pasta and keep on very low heat.
- Add the cooked cauliflower, broccoli and onions, the raisins, sour cherries, parsley and ¼ cup of almonds. Stir to combine, adding some more pasta water if required. Raise the heat slightly, to bring it all together.
- Taste for seasoning.
- Transfer to a bowl, top with chopped parsley, Parmesan and the remaining almonds.
- Serve immediately.

Sesame Cauliflower

Aman took to this dish as a baby when we ate it at a favourite restaurant near our house. The restaurant version is deep-fried and tossed in lots of cornflour. My version cuts back on the frying by caramelising it in the oven and also uses far less processed ingredients. The toasted sesame seeds add a healthy crunch (they are high in calcium). All in all a lovely, healthy recipe.

Time: 40 minutes | Serves: 2-4

Ingredients

Cauliflower

- 1 kg cauliflower, cut into bite-sized florets without stems
- ½ cup + 1 tbsp salt
- ½ cup oil
- ½ cup cornflour

Sauce

- 1 tsp oil
- 1 tsp ginger-garlic paste
- 1 green chilli, minced (optional)
- ½ cup tomato sauce
- 1 tsp rice vinegar
- 2 tsp soy sauce
- 1 tsp cornflour
- ½ cup vegetable stock

Garnish

- ½ cup chopped spring onions
- ½ cup sesame seeds (til), toasted

Method

Cauliflower

- Pour enough water in a pan to immerse the cauliflower. Add ½ cup of salt and place the pan on high heat. Bring to a boil.
- Immerse the cauliflower in the boiling water and boil, till the cauliflower is lightly cooked.
- Strain out and leave to drain on kitchen paper.
- Place the cauliflower in a large bowl. Sprinkle in the oil and 1 tsp of salt and toss till the cauliflower is well coated.
- Place the cauliflower in a single layer on a rimmed baking sheet.
- Using a sieve, lightly dust the florets with a thin film of cornflour.
- Set aside for 2 minutes, so that the flour sticks to the oil-coated cauliflower.
- Bake in the centre of an oven preheated to 180°C for 25-30 minutes. The cauliflower should be nicely browned.

Sauce

- While your cauliflower is in the oven, make the sauce.
- Put the oil in a pan on medium heat. When hot, add the ginger-garlic paste and green chilli. Stir-fry, till fragrant.
- Add the tomato sauce, vinegar and soy sauce.
- Dissolve the cornflour in the stock, mix well and pour it into the pan. Stir, till the sauce is thick.

To serve

- As soon as your cauliflower is out of the oven, toss with the sauce, spring onions and sesame seeds.
- Serve immediately; it really isn't half as delicious if it's been sitting on the counter getting cold.

Rainbow Idlis

Time: 1 hour | Serves: 2-4

Ingredients

Carrot purée

- 1 tbsp olive oil1 cup diced carrots
- ½ tsp sugar
- A pinch of salt

Spinach purée

- 120 gms spinach
- 1 small onion, chopped
- 2 garlic cloves, minced
- A pinch of salt
- ½ tsp freshly grated nutmeg

Beetroot purée

- 1 cup diced beetroot
- A pinch of salt

Moong purée

- 1 cup husked, split moong beans (moong dal)
- ½ tsp turmeric powder
- A pinch of salt

Idlis

- 1 kg idli batter, home-made or store-bought
- Ghee or oil for greasing moulds

Garnish

- ¼ cup finely diced green, red and yellow bell peppers
- ¼ cup cooked green peas
- ¼ cup finely diced carrots
- ¼ cup finely diced French beans, blanched
- ¼ cup cooked sweet corn kernels

Method

Carrot purée

- Put the oil in a pan on medium heat. When hot, sauté the diced carrots for about 5 minutes, till soft.
- Season with sugar and salt.
- Process to a smooth purée in the blender. Reserve.

Spinach purée

- Clean and wash the spinach thoroughly in several changes of water. Drain.
- Steam the spinach with the onion and garlic for about 2 minutes, till bright green.
- Season with nutmeg and salt.
- Process to a smooth purée in the blender. Reserve.

Beetroot purée

- Cook the beetroot in salted water for about 10 minutes, till soft.
- Drain and add a pinch of salt.
- Process to a smooth purée in the blender. Reserve.

Moong purée

- Wash the moong dal.
- Put the dal in a pressure cooker with 1 cup of water.
- Pressure-cook the dal for 10 minutes on low heat, after the cooker reaches full pressure.
- Remove from heat and set aside, till the pressure subsides.
- Add the turmeric powder and salt and process to a smooth purée in the blender. Reserve.

To make the idlis

- Divide the idli batter into four portions.
- Stir a vegetable purée into each portion of batter and combine well, so that you have an orange, green, red and yellow batter. Taste and check for seasoning.
- Grease idli moulds with ghee or oil. (Use mini idli moulds for kids; they love them.)
- Pour the batter into the moulds and arrange a few pieces of the prepared garnishes on top in attractive patterns.
- Steam the idlis for about 10-15 minutes.
- When done, remove the idlis from their moulds and serve.

Best Spaghetti And Meatballs Ever!

It's a standing joke among my friends on Facebook that my status updates make them hungry. But when you are constantly developing or testing recipes for various projects, the line between cooking for work and daily cooking gets blurred. I hate wasting food, so I work out meal plans that allow me to cook things I need to test at regular meals. (And if your kids give something a stamp of approval, you know that recipe is a winner.) I was testing this recipe for a story, but it turned out to be the BEST SPAGHETTI AND MEATBALLS EVER according to my son!

Time: 45 minutes | Serves: 4

Ingredients

- 1 packet (500 gms) spaghetti (you could also use capellini)

Sauce

- ½ cup extra virgin olive oil
- 1 whole garlic bulb, peeled and finely chopped
- 4 onions, finely chopped
- 1 zucchini, finely chopped with skin
- 2 red bell peppers, finely chopped
- 1 tbsp green chilli-garlic paste
- 1 kg can of Italian plum tomatoes (All those chefs that tell you that canned Italian tomatoes are good for a tomato-based sauce? They're spot on! The flavour and colour is phenomenal.)
- ½ tsp sugarSalt to taste
- ⅓ cup grated Parmesan cheese

Meatballs

- ½ cup coriander leaves
- 400 gms chicken, minced

- 2 tbsp finely chopped onion, reserved from the onions sautéed while making the sauce
- ⅓ cup finely chopped garlic
- 1 tsp minced green chilli
- ½ tsp salt
- 1 egg, whisked
- 2 tbsp powdered toasted pistachios

To serve
- ½ cup grated Parmesan cheese

Method

Sauce
- Put a large pan on low heat and pour in the olive oil.
- Add the garlic and onions and give them a quick stir so that they are well coated in oil. When they begin to sweat, take out 2 tbsp of the cooked garlic and onion and reserve them for the meatballs.
- Add the zucchini and bell peppers. Leave them to sweat (not fry, just gently sweat) for about 5 minutes.
- Add the chilli-garlic paste and the can of Italian plum tomatoes.
- Stir and add the sugar and salt. Taste and adjust the seasonings.
- Leave on low heat to cook.

Meatballs
- Wash the coriander leaves thoroughly in several changes of water. Drain well and chop fine.
- Place the mince in a large mixing bowl and mix in the reserved softened garlic and onions.
- Add the finely chopped garlic, coriander leaves, green chilli and salt.
- Stir in the egg and toasted pistachio powder. Mix well and reserve.
- By now your sauce should be boiling away and smelling fabulous.
- Double its volume by adding water so the meatballs have enough space to cook. Bring to a boil again.
- Using a spoon, shape the mince into small balls and drop them into the bubbling sauce.
- Add the Parmesan, reduce the heat and cook uncovered for about 30 minutes,

till the excess moisture dries out.
- The sauce will be a beautiful red, flecked with green from the zucchini and will have thickened to a luscious consistency with a film of red-tinted oil on top.

To serve

- In the meanwhile, cook the spaghetti according to the packet instructions, till al dente (or see page 150).
- Drain and transfer to a serving dish.
- Spoon the meatballs and sauce over the spaghetti and serve with grated Parmesan on the side.

Pinky's Carrot Cake

My friend Pinky's carrot cake recipe. This is a sure fire way to get carrots into kids.

Time: 35 minutes | Makes: 1 cake or 12 small muffins

Ingredients
- 1½ cups refined flour (maida)
- 1½ tsp baking soda
- 1 tsp freshly grated nutmeg
- 2 tsp powdered cinnamon
- ½ tsp salt
- 3 cups grated carrots
- 1½ cups sugar
- 1 cup sunflower oil1 cup chopped walnuts + extra for garnish
- 3 eggs, beaten

Method
- Preheat the oven to 180ºC if you are making a cake or 220ºC for muffins.
- Sift the flour with the baking soda, nutmeg, cinnamon and salt into a bowl.
- Blend the grated carrots, sugar, oil, walnuts and eggs in another bowl.
- Mix the dry ingredients into this mixture.
- Pour the batter into a lightly greased 10" cake tin or 12 muffin moulds.
- Bake the cake in the preheated oven for 15-20 minutes and the muffins for 10-12 minute.
- Turn out on to a wire rack to cool.
- Decorate with the extra walnuts and serve cold or warm.

Buttered Vegetables And Clear Soup

When Aman was a toddler, I made it a rule to feed him ahead of our evening meal. I would then have him 'join' us for dinner, giving him something easy to eat by himself. At that age kids love doing things on their own and this colourful mix was something that kept him busy and exposed him to a variety of vegetables, according to availability.

Time: 25 minutes | Serves: 2

Ingredients
- 1 tsp salt
- ½ cup shelled green peas
- ½ cup diced French beans
- 1 cup diced carrots
- 1 cup diced potatoes
- ½ tsp butter
- Freshly ground black pepper to taste

Method
- Pour 2 cups of water into a deep pan and add the salt. Bring the water to a boil on high heat.
- Add each vegetable separately to the pan and cook, till the colour brightens and the vegetable is cooked through but firm to the touch.
- Remove the vegetable with a slotted spoon, as it is cooked and transfer to a bowl.
- Add half the butter into the soup and reserve.
- Mix the remaining butter into the vegetables. Taste and add more salt, if required.
- Keep some of the cooked vegetables aside for your baby and add the rest to the soup in the pan. Heat through and add salt and pepper to taste.
- Serve as a nutritious clear soup to the baby and others in the family.

India on My Plate

India is ancient, with a culture that is centuries old. The roots of Indian cuisine were sown when the geographical borders of the Indian subcontinent were drawn, spanning many climate zones, home to a variety of flora and fauna and indigenous ingredients that were harvested by the ancient civilisations of India. As these civilisations grew, settlements branched out over the subcontinent taking with them their foodways and adapting them to what was available locally. With no unifying modes of communication and days of travel between settlements, there was little, if any, contact between them. Each developed an autonomous culture, with clothes, lifestyles and even food evolving into local Kashmiri, Gujarati, Bengali or Tamil cuisines rather than a pan-Indian one.

This regional diversity prevailed down the ages, and was enriched as cuisines bifurcated and merged, incorporating new ingredients, foodways and culinary influences of invaders, settlers and new religions to Muslim, Portuguese, Jewish, French, British, Parsi, Sindhi and East Indian were stirred into the delicious mix so that today, Indian cuisine changes every few hundred kilometers (if not less!) as you traverse the country.

So, what brings everything together as 'Indian'? The answer comes easily. Imagine a Sambhar without the characteristic fragrance of curry leaves. Or (God forbid) a Bengali Shorshe Ilish without mustard! The defining factor in Indian cooking is the use of spices. The essence of Indian cooking revolves around a skilled, subtle blending of appropriate spices. This blending is rooted in the Vedas and has been passed down the ages. The objective of using spices has always been to enhance rather than overwhelm the basic flavour of a particular dish as well as to augment its nutritional qualities, no matter if the dish in question is savoury or sweet!

It would take a lifetime and many meals to just complete sampling one's way through the vastness of Indian cuisine! Thankfully, however, I live in Mumbai, a metropolis that has all of India on its menu of its own. Something I realised rather late in life!

Thencha-inspired Pesto

Traditional thencha is all about the heat but this green bell pepper version ups the green chilli flavour and mutes the heat slightly. It is great to toss pasta in.

Time: 15 minutes | Makes: 1 cup of pesto

Ingredients
- 500 gms green bell peppers, kept whole
- 125 gms green chillies, kept whole
- 12 garlic cloves, kept whole
- Oil as required
- 2 tbsp rock salt

Method
- Arrange the bell peppers, green chillies and garlic cloves in a small baking tray.
- Drizzle with oil and roast uniformly on all sides, till you see brown-black spots over them.
- Place the roasted bell peppers in a paper bag to sweat off the skins. Peel and reserve. Place the peeled bell peppers, roasted chillies and garlic in a mortar and pestle or blender with the salt and process to make a coarse paste.

Zhanzhanit Maharashtrian Mirchi Thencha
(Pounded Chilli Chutney)

Zhanzhanit, meaning electrifyingly spicy in Marathi, is a word used exclusively for chilli preparations, mainly those that are so hot they make one cry while eating them!

Every region in India has a different variety and a local variant of a simple chilli paste to spice things up. In Maharashtra, this chilli condiment is the thencha (literally meaning pounded, owing to its method of preparation). The flavour we get from spices comes from the inherent oils present in them that are released when the plant is endangered. And there is nothing like a good pounding to make those chillies good and angry! The smoky flavour from the roasting adds to the heat of the chillies and the aroma of the garlic.

Thencha is good to make and have on hand, because it can augment daily cooking in several ways. Stir it into anything to add fire, serve it as a condiment or toss it with potatoes as I have done below, or prawns, chicken or just about anything for a handy side dish or starter. I recommend using a mortar and pestle to pound it. Thencha can be stored for 4-5 days in the refrigerator.

Time: 15 minutes | Makes: 1/3 cup of chutney

Ingredients
- 6-10 hot, spicy green chillies, kept whole
- 12 garlic cloves, kept whole
- 1 tsp oil
- 1 tbsp chunky rock salt

Method
- Roast the chillies and garlic on an open flame or in a pan with oil, till you see

brown-black spots over them.
- Cool and grind in a mortar and pestle or blender with the salt and to make a coarse paste.

Thencha Potatoes

A great side dish or starter, or even a quick meal!

Time: 20 minutes | Serves: 4

Ingredients
- 4-5 potatoes
- 1 tbsp oil
- 2 tbsp thencha (page 202)
- ½ cup stock or water
- Salt to taste
- 2 tbsp chopped coriander leaves

Method
- Scrub the potatoes and parboil them in their jackets.
- Peel or leave the skin on, and cut into chunks.
- Alternatively, cut the potatoes into chunks and deep-fry, till half cooked.
- Put the oil in a pan on medium heat. When hot, add the thencha and sauté for 30 seconds.
- Pour in the stock or water to break up the paste into a sauce.
- Add salt to taste.
- Add the potatoes and toss them well, till they are coated with the oil.
- Taste and adjust seasoning if required.
- Sprinkle with coriander leaves and stir-fry for about 5 minutes, till the potatoes are tender and crisp on the outside.

Winnie Aunty's Sprout Salad

Winnie Aunty was first my Dad's and later my Mom's personal assistant and was part of our lives for most of my growing years. I remember her most for two reasons: the aroma of the fresh-ground Mangalorean filter coffee she picked up every fortnight from Phillips Coffee down the road, and the many delicious treats, such as bread puddings, guava cheese and yummy cakes, she brought us. She discovered sprouted fenugreek and concocted this salad when she was diagnosed as borderline diabetic. The sweet crunchy sprouted masoor and apple play an ideal backdrop to the slightly bitter fenugreek.

Time: 20 minutes | Serves: 4

Ingredients
- 1 apple, chopped
- 1 cup whole Egyptian lentils (sabut masoor) sprouts
- ½ cup fenugreek seed sprouts (methi)
- 1 small onion, finely chopped
- 1 medium-sized tomato, finely chopped
- 1 green chilli, finely chopped
- Juice of 1 lime
- Salt to taste

Method
- Combine everything in a large mixing bowl and toss.
- Taste and add more salt, if required.

Sindhi Curry
(Piquant Tomato and Gram Flour Curry)

Despite its huge presence in Mumbai, I was first introduced to the addictive Sindhi cuisine very late in life, with the advent of my sister-in-law Sheetal into our family. She opened up the wonderful world of Sindhi food for me. This dish is a Sindhi speciality — a spicy mixed vegetable dish served with pao or rice as a Sunday meal.

Time: 1 hour | Serves: 4

Ingredients
- ½ cup husked, split pigeon peas (toover/arhar dal)
- 3 medium-sized tomatoes, halved
- 3 tbsp oil
- ¾ tsp cumin seeds
- ¼ tsp fenugreek seeds (methi)
- A pinch of asafoetida powder (hing)
- 2-3 green chillies, slit
- 7-8 curry leaves
- 3 tbsp gram flour (besan)
- 6-8 small okra (bhindi), trimmed and slit
- 70 gms cluster beans (gwar phalli), trimmed
- 1 tsp red chilli powder
- ¼ tsp turmeric powder
- 2-3 drumsticks, cut into 2" segments
- Salt to taste
- 2 tbsp tamarind pulp

Method
- Wash the dal and soak it in 2 cups of water for about 30 minutes.
- Drain the dal and put it in a pressure cooker with the tomatoes and 2 cups of

water. Pressure-cook the dal for 10 minutes on low heat, after the cooker reaches full pressure.
- Remove from heat and set aside, till the pressure subsides.
- When cool, mash the dal and press it through a strainer into a bowl.
- Put the oil in a heavy-bottomed pan on medium heat. When hot, add the cumin seeds, fenugreek seeds and asafoetida powder.
- When the cumin seeds begin to change colour, add the green chillies and curry leaves and fry for 30 seconds.
- Add the gram flour and roast for about 5 minutes, till it turns reddish brown.
- Pour in 3 cups of water, a little at a time and keep stirring to avoid lumps.
- Add the okra and cluster beans and sauté for 3 minutes.
- Mix in the mashed dal, chilli powder, turmeric powder, drumsticks and salt to taste and bring to a boil.
- Add a little water to the tamarind pulp and pour it into the kadhi. Mix well.
- Serve hot with steamed white rice.

Yasmin's Bohri Chana Bateta

Chana bateta was something Yasmin, one of the office girls, brought for lunch often. I forgot about it, till I tried it a few years later, thanks to my friend Rita D'Souza who is an aficionado of all things culinary and author of two cookbooks ('Goan Kitchen' and 'Pickles and Chutneys of India'). Rita also introduced me to pyaali, a street version of chana bateta that is found in the busy streets of Bohri Mohalla in Bhendi Bazaar.

Time: 45 minutes + overnight for soaking | Serves: 4

Ingredients
- 2 cups whole Bengal gram/black garbanzo beans (kala chana)
- 1 tsp salt
- 1 medium-sized potato
- 2 tbsp gram flour (besan)
- 3 tbsp oil
- 1 tsp cumin seeds
- 1 onion, finely chopped
- 1 green chilli, finely chopped
- 1 tsp ginger-garlic paste
- 1 tbsp tamarind, soaked in 1 tbsp warm water
- 1 tbsp jaggery dissolved in 1 tbsp warm water

Garnish
- 1 tbsp chopped coriander leaves
- 2 small onions, chopped
- A handful (30 gms) of fresh mint leaves, chopped

Method
- Wash the gram and soak it in water overnight.

- In the morning, rinse the gram well.
- Put the gram in a pressure cooker. Add salt and 4 cups of water.
- Pressure-cook for 15-20 minutes on low heat, after the cooker reaches full pressure.
- Remove from heat and set aside, till the pressure subsides. The gram should be soft enough to bite, but not mushy.
- Strain, reserving the water and gram.
- Boil the potato, peel and dice it.
- Prepare a paste of the gram flour with a little water in a small bowl, ensuring it has no lumps.
- Put half the oil in a small pan on high heat. When hot, add the cumin seeds. Cook, till a little past the crackling stage.
- Once they are turning slightly brown, reduce the heat to medium and add the gram flour paste. Stir and remove from heat.
- Put the remaining oil in another pan on medium heat. When hot, add the onion and green chilli and stir-fry, till the onion is soft.
- Add the ginger-garlic paste and sauté for a minute.
- Stir in the boiled gram with half the reserved cooking liquid.
- Add the potato and gram flour paste, stirring continuously. If you want the gravy thinner, adjust the consistency by adding more of the reserved cooking liquid.
- Squeeze the tamarind pulp through a strainer into the pan and mix in the jaggery. Cook for about 5 minutes, till it starts boiling.
- Remove from heat.
- Garnish with coriander leaves, onions and mint leaves and serve.

Lora's Goan Sausage Pulao

Lora, one of the other girls at the office, loved sausage pulao. She brought it for lunch very often and I developed a fondness for it. It's been on our menu since then, whenever we get our hands on good spicy Goan sausage.

Time: 45 minutes | Serves: 4

Ingredients
- 3 cups basmati rice
- 200 gms Goan sausages
- 2 tbsp vegetable oil
- 1 large onion, finely sliced
- 4 cloves
- 2 x 1" cinnamon sticks
- 4 green cardamom pods
- 1 large tomato, finely sliced
- 3 chicken, beef or vegetable stock cubes
- ½ cup shelled green peas
- Salt to taste

Method
- Wash the rice and soak it in water for 30 minutes to an hour.
- Pressure-cook the sausages with just enough water to cover for 15 minutes on low heat, after the cooker reaches full pressure.
- Remove from heat and set aside, till the pressure subsides.
- Remove and discard the skins of the sausages. Cut the sausages into halves. Reserve.
- Put the oil in a pan on medium heat. When hot, sauté the onion and whole spices, till the onion is golden.
- Add the tomato and sauté, till it turns mushy.
- Crumble in the stock cubes.

- Drain the rice and add it to the pan. Stir-fry, till the rice is coated with the contents of the pan.
- Pour in 6 cups of warm water and add the green peas.
- Taste and add more salt, if required.
- Cover the pan and simmer on low heat, till the rice is half cooked.
- Place half the sausages over the rice. Reduce the heat to very low and simmer, till the water has dried and rice is tender and fluffy.
- Remove from heat and spoon on to a serving platter.
- Garnish with the remaining sausages and serve.

Zarine's Parsi Papeta Per Eeda
(Eggs over Potatoes)

Zarine was another lovely lady I worked with. The Parsis love eggs and a favourite way of cooking them is to top any vegetable with them. Papeta per eeda, is like a frittata — spicy potatoes topped with eggs — but you can use any vegetable in place of potatoes, even okra, which Zarine is particularly fond of.

Time: 15 minutes | Serves: 2

Ingredients
- 2-3 tbsp oil
- ½ tsp mustard seeds
- ½ tsp asafoetida powder (hing)
- 2 small green chillies, cut into halves
- 6-7 curry leaves
- ¼ tsp turmeric powder
- 4-5 medium-sized potatoes, sliced
- 1 tbsp grated fresh ginger (optional)
- ⅓ tsp + ⅓ tsp salt
- ¼ cup finely chopped coriander leaves
- 3 eggs + 3 egg whites

Method
- Put the oil in a pan on medium heat. When hot, add the mustard seeds.
- As they start to crackle, add the asafoetida powder, followed by the green chillies, curry leaves and turmeric powder.
- Add the potatoes and mix gently.
- Stir in the ginger (if using) and then ⅓ tsp of salt.
- Cover and cook on medium heat, till the potatoes are tender, but firm.
- Mix in the coriander leaves.

- Break the eggs into a bowl, add the remaining salt and beat, till fluffy.
- Pour the eggs over the cooked potatoes.
- Cover and cook for 4-5 minutes, till the eggs are just set.

Usha's Maa Ki Dal
(Slow-simmered Black Gram)

Usha was my neighbour for a while. Our sons were the same age and are both named Aman. We spent many afternoons gossiping over tea while our kids played, till she moved away. I learnt this recipe from her and it is the best maa ki dal I have eaten. I remember her fondly whenever I make it.

Time: 1¾ hours | Serves: 4-6

Ingredients
- 2 cups mixed whole black gram (urad), kidney beans (rajma) and Bengal gram (kala chana)
- Salt to taste
- ½ tsp red chilli powder
- 6 tomatoes, finely chopped
- 1 cup fresh cream
- 1 tsp garam masala powder
- 1 tbsp finely chopped coriander leaves

Tempering
- 1 tbsp ghee
- 2 onions, finely chopped
- ½ tsp mustard seeds
- 2 tsp ginger-garlic paste

Method
- Wash the mixed dals and pressure-cook them with the salt, chilli powder and 2½ cups of water for at least 30 minutes on low heat, after the cooker reaches full pressure.
- Remove from heat and set aside, till the pressure subsides.
- Blend the tomatoes and cream in a mixer.

- Pour it into the dal.
- Cook on low heat for 20-22 minutes, till the dals are properly cooked.
- Put the ghee for the tempering in a skillet on medium heat. When hot, sauté the onions, till they turn light brown.
- Add the mustard seeds and ginger-garlic paste and sauté for 4 minutes. Pour the contents of the pan over the dal and mix well.
- Add the garam masala powder and coriander leaves and cook for 5 minutes longer before serving.

Aloo Chenchki
(Nigella-scented Potatoes)

My repertoire of Bengali recipes is small, because I have Mita, who I can coerce into cooking for me at any time. Aloo chenchki is the first Bengali dish I learned to cook and the reason I will forever associate kalaunji or nigella seeds with Bengali food. A virtual foodie friend, Gautam, taught me this on www.anothersubcontinent.com as a start in lessons in Bengali cooking. Unfortunately, I lost touch and the lessons ended but the recipe stayed with me. In Gautam's words: 'The thing about my version of Bengali cooking is that much of it is vegetarian and deals with very humble ingredients. Care and skill are paramount.'

Time: 40 minutes | Serves: 4

Ingredients
- 2 tbsp ghee
- 1 tbsp nigella seeds (kalaunji)
- 4 medium potatoes, peeled and cubed
- Salt to taste
- ½ tsp sugar

Method
- Put the ghee in a heavy-bottomed pan or wok (not Teflon) that can be covered.
- When the ghee shimmers and is about to smoke, add the nigella seeds.
- Just as they swim and release their fragrance, add the potatoes. Stir briskly to mix them in.
- Adjust the heat so that the potatoes do not scorch. Stir, till the cubes are shiny and beginning to turn translucent on the outside.
- Stir in the salt and sugar, cover, reduce the heat and cook, till the potatoes are tender.
- When done, the potatoes should have disintegrated just a little, and taste

salty-sweet. You should be able to distinctly taste and smell the aroma of the nigella.
- Serve with rotis.

Kalyan's Doi Posto Eelish
(Hilsa in a Poppy Seed and Yoghurt Gravy)

This recipe comes from my friend Kalyan Karmarkar aka The Knife who is a fellow food blogger and blogs at 'Finely Chopped'. Kalyan often says he is proud of this recipe as it harmonises the two cooking traditions of Bengal: the Bangla (East Bengal) love for hilsa (eelish) and the Ghoti (West Bengal) love for posto. A light, cool, heady poppy base, tempered with a little yoghurt results in a gravy paste that is soothing, pleasant and deliciously flavoured. You could also choose to steam the fish instead, in which case you will need to microwave it for 8 instead of 4 minutes. Serve with steamed white rice and green chillies.

Time: 40 minutes | Serves: 2-4

Ingredients
- 6 pieces of hilsa (shad)
- 1 tsp turmeric powder
- 1 tsp salt
- 2 tbsp oil

Marinade
- A handful (30 gms) of coriander leaves
- 50-75 gms poppy seeds (khus-khus)
- 2 tbsp yoghurt, whisked smooth
- ½ tsp sugar
- ½ tsp coriander powder
- ½ tsp cumin powder

Method
- Wash the fish and pat dry.
- Smear it with the turmeric powder and salt.

- Heat the oil in a frying pan on medium heat. When hot, shallow-fry the fish for less than a minute on both sides, till it just turns opaque. Drain and reserve.
- Wash the coriander leaves for the marinade thoroughly in several changes of water. Drain well and chop fine.
- Combine the marinade ingredients in a small bowl.
- Put the fish in a microwave cooking bowl and add the marinade. Mix, till the fish is well coated with the marinade.
- Leave for 15-30 minutes so the fish can soak in the marinade.
- Put the bowl with the fish and the marinade in a microwave oven on high for 2 minutes. Switch off and take the bowl out.
- Gently turn the fish pieces over. Return to the oven for 2 minutes longer. The fish should now be tender.
- Serve with steamed white rice.

Ross' Momos Or Pot Stickers

Momos are a type of dumpling, believed to be a traditional delicacy of Tibet, but have now become part of the local food culture in the subcontinent. They are also a popular street food in several Indian cities. Though traditional momos are made of meat, in India one finds a variety of vegetarian fillings improvised to suit local tastes.

This recipe is my friend Roshan Tamang's version.

Time: 1½ hours | Serves: 6

Ingredients

Filling

- 250 gms mutton, beef, chicken or pork, finely minced
- 1 tbsp vegetable oil (if required)
- 250 gms onions, finely chopped
- 1" piece of fresh ginger, finely chopped
- Salt to taste
- 2-3 garlic cloves, finely chopped

Dough

- 1 kg refined flour (maida)

Tomato sauce

- 2 ripe tomatoes
- 5-10 dried red chillies, soaked in warm water
- 2 cups coriander leaves
- Salt to taste

Method

Filling

- Mix the filling ingredients in a large bowl. If the meat is lean, add oil to prevent the filling from getting too dry when cooked. (For vegetable fillings, butter is added.) Let the mixture marinate for a while.

Dough
- Sift the flour for the dough into another bowl. Add a little water at a time and knead to make a smooth, consistent dough. Don't make it too hard or too soft. Cover with a damp cloth, to prevent the surface from drying out.

To assemble and cook the momos
- Roll the dough into small rotis, like mini-puris. Try and keep the size and thickness consistent. Remember: too thin and the filling will poke out, too thick and the floury taste takes over.
- Put a spoonful of the filling in the centre of a roti. Bring the dough over the filling to cover it completely. Pinch the edges of the dough to give it a curved shape or a rounded dumpling-like form. Repeat with the remaining rotis and filling.
- Bring water to a boil in a momo cooker. Place the momos on a well-oiled container and steam for 15 minutes. Alternatively, place the momos in a well-oiled colander and steam them over boiling water for 15 minutes.

Tomato sauce
- Boil the tomatoes in water, till well cooked.
- Alternatively, poke them with toothpicks and roast them over a gas stove, till the peel is charred and the flesh is cooked.
- Peel the tomatoes and grind them with the drained red chillies to make a smooth paste.
- Wash the coriander leaves thoroughly in several changes of water. Drain well and chop fine.
- Sprinkle them over the sauce.

To serve
- Arrange the momos and sauce on a plate and serve hot.

Kacchhe Kheeme Ke Kabab
(Minced Mutton Kababs)

This is a speciality of Pushy Aunty's. I met Isha Anand, my best friend during my Mayo years, the day I visited the school for the first time with my family after admissions. We hit it off instantly, there were so many portents (or so we thought) that we were destined to be best friends. We shared our birth month, we had identical watches (blue and white striped Swatches) and our first crushes also shared a birth month! Isha's mother, Pushy Aunty, sent these with her on our train journeys back to school.

Time: 40 minutes | Makes: 30-40 kababs

Ingredients
- 1 cup mint leaves
- 1 cup coriander leaves
- 1 kg mutton, minced
- 2 medium-sized onions, finely diced
- 3 green chillies, finely chopped
- ½ cup cream
- ½ tsp black pepper powder
- 1 tsp salt
- Oil for deep-frying

Method
- Wash the leaves thoroughly in several changes of water. Drain well and chop fine.
- Mix all the ingredients, except the oil for frying, in a bowl. Knead properly for about 5 minutes.
- Divide into small portions and roll into balls about 2"- 3" in diameter.
- Heat the oil in a frying pan and deep-fry the kababs on medium heat, till cooked through and golden brown.
- Serve hot with green mint and lime chutney.

Thukpa Or Gya Thuk In Tibetan
(Noodle Soup)

Time: 30 minutes | Serves: 4

Ingredients
- 200 gms noodles
- 2 tbsp oil
- 5 garlic cloves, finely chopped
- 1" piece of fresh ginger, finely chopped
- 250 gms chicken, minced
- 200 gms chopped mushrooms and baby corn
- A pinch of salt
- 8 cups chicken stock
- 1 tbsp chopped coriander leaves

Method
- Boil the noodles in salted water, till tender, but firm.
- Drain and rinse under running cold water.
- Toss the cooked noodles with 1 tsp of oil so that the strands do not stick to each other. Set aside. Put the remaining oil in a pan on medium heat. When hot, fry the garlic, ginger, chicken, mushrooms and baby corn lightly, till cooked.
- Mix in the salt and reserve.
- Bring the stock to a rolling boil in another pan.
- Divide the noodles into 4 bowls and pour the hot stock over them.
- Garnish with the chicken mix and coriander leaves.
- Serve hot.

Culinary Souviners

There's something empowering about a holiday. It utterly transforms you. You turn up in a new place not knowing anything from anything, unable to get your tongue around the names for the simplest dishes, let alone tell anyone what they are. Yet by the time you leave, you can hold forth with confidence about the everyday meal of that country, its culinary influences and pronounce the names of everything … well almost! This connection between food and travel is natural. Food is an instant memory prompter, a single bite or whiff is enough to carry you instantly to happy times. Food is the most accessible medium to explore the traditions and cultures of countries we travel to.

The best way to discover a place is through its food. Looking for interesting dining experiences and the search for culinary souvenirs will open up new doors in terms of discovering a place, while generating lots of grist for the mill of dinner table conversations back home. 'Culinary souvenirs' is a term I coined later in life to encompass all these little pieces of my holidays attached to the memory of great dining experiences. Knickknacks that effectively bridge the gap between wanting a tangible piece of that particular flavour of heaven and the practicality of returning to home and life!

When food is in my mouth, the flavours are of course paramount, but even as my palate is savouring the taste, my mind relishes all the little details I associate with it. Most often it is about the stories and memories attached to the food I cook and eat that make me passionate about it. But it is not just the eating that I relish, I love the entire process of cooking something associated with an exotic locale or a great dining experience. Assembling the ingredients, prepping them, losing myself in the smells and textures of the ingredients as I prepare them and reliving the experience of discovering the dish itself as I cook, preserves the memories as no photograph could.

Culinary souvenirs can be anything: from those that cost you every last bit of your travel allowance like Le Crueset you picked up in Paris (French Le Crueset cookware is valued by cooks the world over and passed down in families) or cost nothing, like a paper napkin from the day you tasted Berry Pulao at Britannia and Co. in Bombay (embellished with a picture of their mascot, the owner's pet rooster, and proclaiming 'There is no love greater than the love of eating'), or—as in my case—they could be recipes.

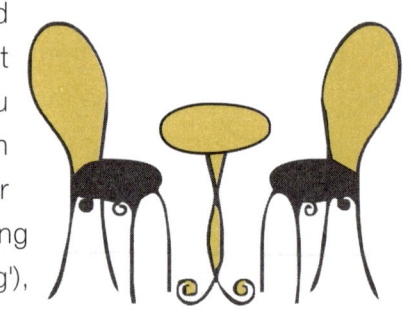

Mexican Potato Salad

Time: 30 minutes | Serves: 4

Ingredients
- 1 kg potatoes, boiled, peeled and cut into chunks
- 2 tbsp white wine vinegar
- 1 tbsp minced pickled jalapeño peppers
- 2 tbsp pickled jalapeño pepper brine
- 2 tbsp olive oil or vegetable oil
- 3 celery sticks, finely sliced
- ½ cup finely chopped onion
- ¼ tsp freshly ground black pepper

Method
- Combine all the ingredients in a bowl and mix well.
- Taste and adjust seasoning.
- Serve at room temperature, or slightly chilled.

My Sister Himanshi's Prawn Curry

My sister Himanshi is the sort of girl that never cooked while growing up, subsisting on Maggi, chocolate and chai. I have marvelled at how the little tomboy that was always scraped knees, crooked pigtails and tanned skinniness can today address a room full of people with utmost grace and poise. Like everything else, she has developed into a fairly good cook after marriage. This is a recipe she created. According to her it's 'excellent for when you are craving a curry but don't really want to eat chicken again'.

Time: 25 minutes | Serves: 4

Ingredients

- 700 gms prawns, shelled, tails removed and deveined

Marinade

- Juice of 1 lime
- ⅓ tsp salt

Curry

- 1 tsp oil
- 1" cinnamon stick
- 1" piece of fresh ginger, grated
- 3-4 garlic cloves, finely chopped
- 4 small onions, chopped
- 3 large tomatoes, finely chopped
- ½ tsp red chilli powder (optional)
- 1 tsp garam masala powder
- ½ tsp coriander-cumin powder
- ⅓ tsp salt
- ½ cup thin coconut milk

Method

- Wash the prawns and drain thoroughly.
- Mix the marinade ingredients in a bowl and rub it into the prawns.
- Put the oil in a kadhai or wok on medium heat. When hot, sauté the cinnamon, ginger and garlic for a minute.
- Add the onions and sauté, till golden brown. Mix in the tomatoes, spice powders and salt. Sprinkle in a little water if required and stir and cook, till the tomatoes are soft and mushy.
- Remove the pan from the heat.
- Blend the cooked mixture in a food processor, till it forms a purée.
- Return the purée to the same pan on medium heat and add the prawns.
- Mix well to ensure that the prawns are well coated in the gravy. Stir often and cook for 2-3 minutes, till the prawns curl up and turn pink.
- Pour in the coconut milk, stir to mix well and cook for 2 minutes longer.
- Serve with hot steamed white rice.

Sheetal's Prawn Curry In Green Masala

Sheetal is my sister-in-law. In her I found many things — a sister much closer to me in age; a friend that did not have to go home at the end of the day (just to the other room); a conspirator in cooking capers and most especially, a woman I admire. This is one of my favourite dishes by her.

Time: 45 minutes | Serves: 4

Ingredients

Spice paste

- 200 gms coriander leaves
- ½ cup chopped garlic
- 1" piece of fresh ginger, chopped
- A handful (30 gms) of fresh mint leaves
- 4-5 spicy green chillies

Curry

- 2 tbsp oil
- 1 cup chopped white onions
- 1 tbsp garam masala powder
- 500 gms large prawns, cleaned and deveined
- 1 cup thick coconut milk
- Salt to taste

Garnish

- 2 tbsp chopped coriander leaves

Method

- Wash the coriander leaves thoroughly in several changes of water. Drain well and chop.
- Grind the spice paste ingredients to a smooth consistency. Set aside.

- Put the oil in a pan on medium heat. When hot, sauté the onions, till translucent.
- Add the spice paste, garam masala powder, prawns and coconut milk. Give it a stir.
- Add salt to taste, stir well and simmer, till the prawns just curl up.
- Garnish with coriander leaves and serve the curry with steamed basmati rice.

South African Bunny Chow Recipe À La Rushina

Bunny chow is slang for a South African fast food in which a loaf of bread, is scooped out and filled with a curry. This dish was created in Durban, during the 1940s, allegedly by the Indian 'bania' (therefore bunny) community that settled there). Bunny chow was a means of serving take-away without the need for cutlery to other ethnic communities the banias were not allowed to fraternise with. Make extra — it is even better for breakfast the next day with garam chai! Great party food because you eat the bowl, so no washing up!

Time: 1 hour | Serves: 4-6

Ingredients
- 2 tbsp vegetable oil
- 1" cinnamon stick
- 3-4 hot green chillies, slit
- 4-5 curry leaves
- 1 small onion, sliced
- 1½ tsp ginger paste
- 1½ tsp garlic paste
- 1 kg boneless chicken (though lamb is great too), cut into bite-sized pieces
- 6 small potatoes, cubed
- 2 cups red kidney beans (rajma),cooked
- 4 medium-sized tomatoes, cut into chunks
- 4 tbsp Kitchen King powder (The original recipe calls for Durban masala but I use Kitchen King)
- 3 tbsp red chilli powder
- Salt to taste
- 2 large or 6 small kadak pao

Garnish
- 2 tbsp chopped coriander leaves

Method

- Put the oil in a deep pan on medium heat. When hot, add the cinnamon, green chillies, curry leaves and onion and sauté, till the onion is light golden.
- Add the ginger and garlic and stir-fry for 1 minute.
- Add the chicken and cook for about 10 minutes, stirring all the while, till well browned.
- Add the potatoes and kidney beans and cook for 3-4 minutes.
- Stir in the tomatoes and simmer, till they are mushy.
- Sprinkle in the spice powders, salt and pour in ¼ cup of water. Mix well.
- Cook on medium heat, stirring occasionally, till the chicken and potatoes are tender. Add some water if required, to prevent burning.
- Taste and adjust seasoning.
- Simmer for a further 10 minutes on low heat.
- Slice the tops off the pao and scoop out the soft white bread, leaving the crust to form a 'bowl'.
- Spoon the curry into this bread 'bowl' and garnish with coriander leaves.
- Serve hot. The soft crumbs can be dipped into the curry and eaten as well.

Hainanese Chicken Rice

Whenever I research the food of any place, I visit the local markets. Local markets are powerful places; they have an energy that is addictive and one gets to see all sorts of ingredients. In Singapore I visited what is locally called a wet market, and discovered several wonderful and new ingredients that day but I will always remember my visit for the Hainanese chicken rice we ate for lunch on our way out.

Time: 1 hour | Serves: 4-6

Ingredients

Chicken

- 1 (about 1¼ kg) chicken, whole or cut
- 2-3 heads (300 gms) pak choy or spinach, washed
- 1 tsp salt
- 1 large onion, sliced
- 4 slices fresh ginger
- 1-2 green chillies, pounded

Rice

- 2 tbsp vegetable oil
- 8 garlic cloves, minced
- 4 cups long-grained rice, washed and drained
- 1 tsp salt

Chilli sauce

- 2-3 tbsp lime juice, freshly squeezed
- 5 tbsp fresh red chillies, finely chopped
- 5 garlic cloves, minced
- 3 tbsp grated fresh ginger
- 1 tsp salt

- ½ cup boiling hot chicken broth

Method
Chicken
- Wash the chicken thoroughly and drain.
- Wash the pak choy or spinach thoroughly in several changes of water. Drain.
- Bring water to boil in a large pan with the salt.
- If you are using a whole chicken stuff it with the onion, ginger and green chillies and put it into the boiling water, breast-side down.
- If you are using pieces add the chicken and the these ingredients to the water.
- Bring the water to a boil again, reduce the heat, cover the pan and simmer, till the chicken is just cooked (35 minutes for whole chicken, less for the cut pieces).
- Put the pak choy or spinach leaves in a strainer and lower it into the boiling soup for a few minutes, till bright green and tender.
- Remove the strainer from the broth and set aside.
- Remove the chicken from the broth, drain and rinse in ice-cold water. Drain and slice the chicken flesh. Strain the broth. Reserve the chicken and the broth.

Rice
- Put the oil for the rice in a large pan on medium heat. When hot, add the garlic and stir-fry, till fragrant.
- Add the rice and stir-fry for 2 minutes.
- Mix in the salt.
- Ladle in enough chicken broth to come ½" above the rice and boil on high heat.
- Once the water has dried out, cover the pan and steam on low heat for about 30 minutes, till the rice is cooked.

Chilli sauce
- Combine all the ingredients for the chilli sauce and mix well.
- Serve the rice with the sliced chicken, pak choy or spinach, chilli sauce and hot chicken broth to wash it down.

Lonavala Baked Beans

My grandfather bought the Nawab of Lonavala's beautiful palace eons ago and generations of our family have grown up tripping over the roots of the ancient trees in its orchard, skinning our knees on the gravel of the red earth. It is a rich heritage of memories that he made possible for us that I am sad to say my children will probably not really experience thanks to the vagaries of family property disputes. But life is about change. And while I cannot do anything to carry the legacy of Lonavala forward to my kids, I can take this dish, that we always ate in Lonavala and I made on a holiday in Goa and often in Dehra Dun. They taste just as good, seasoned with memories and spiced with stories of Lonavala!

Time: 30 minutes | Serves: 4

Ingredients
- 1 tbsp oil
- 1 medium-sized onion, finely chopped
- 5-6 garlic cloves, finely sliced
- 1 green chilli, finely chopped
- 1 can (250 gms) baked beans
- 1 tbsp tomato ketchup or as required
- 1 tbsp red chilli sauce or as required
- 3 tbsp grated processed Cheddar cheese

Method
- Put the oil in a pan on medium heat. When hot, add the onion, garlic and green chilli and sauté, till the onion is translucent and just browning at the edges.
- Add the baked beans and mix.
- Stir in the tomato ketchup and chilli sauce.
- Mix in the cheese and remove from heat.
- Serve hot with buttered pao or toast.

Cindy's Porridge Or Congee

This porridge is my personal instant version of Chinese congee that I invented using beaten rice and a flavourful home-made stock. Redolent of ginger, spicy with chillies and topped with a selection of relishes to add accents of delicious flavour to each bite.

Time: 20 minutes | Serves: 2

Ingredients

- 1 tbsp oil
- 1 cup diced chicken or vegetables (celery, carrot, beans and mushrooms), finely chopped, or a combination
- 9 cups chicken or vegetable stock
- Salt to taste
- 2 cups white or unpolished thick beaten rice (jada poha)
- A few generous twists of freshly ground black pepper

Accompaniments

- ⅓ cup chilli oil,
- ⅓ cup finely sliced fresh red or green chillies
- ⅓ cup finely sliced spring onion greens
- A handful (30 gms) of fresh Thai basil leaves

Method

- Put the oil in a large pan on medium heat. When hot, add the chicken or vegetables and sauté lightly, till well coated in oil and almost cooked.
- Pour in the stock and add salt to taste. Bring to a boil on high heat.
- Add the rice and cook, till the porridge has achieved the desired thickness.
- Mix in the pepper, taste and adjust salt.
- Put the accompaniments in individual bowls and serve them on the side with the congee.

Pho
(Vietnamese Noodle Soup with Chicken)

The ultimate comfort food, this soup is delicate but filling, fragrant and satisfying — and historically interesting. Phô means 'your own bowl', that is, something that you garnish and eat individually, not to be shared, as most other Vietnamese dishes customarily are.

Time: 45 minutes | Serves: 4

Ingredients

- 2 (400 gms) boneless chicken breasts, kept whole
- ½ tsp salt
- ½ tsp freshly ground black pepper
- 1 tbsp lime juice
- 8 cups light chicken or vegetable stock
- 1 tbsp ginger-garlic paste
- 150 gms rice noodles (rice sticks or egg noodles)

Accompaniments

- ¼ cup finely sliced spring onion greens
- ½ cup fresh basil leaves
- 2 cusp fresh bean sprouts
- 6 lime slices
- 2 tbsp finely sliced chillies
- 2-3 tbsp fish sauce

Method

- Season chicken breasts with salt, pepper and lime juice and reserve.
- Put the stock and, ginger-garlic paste in a large pan on high heat and bring to a boil.
- Add the chicken breasts and cook for exactly 12 minutes, by which time they will turn white and opaque. Remove the chicken from the pan and reserve.

- Add the noodles to the pan and boil, till cooked.
- Strain and reserve the noodles and broth.
- Meanwhile slice the chicken.
- Arrange the accompaniments in individual bowls and put the bowls on a platter.
- Distribute the noodles between 4 soup bowls, top with chicken and hot broth.
- Serve immediately, with the platter of accompaniments on the side.

Variation: To make a vegetarian version, use 400 gms of quartered mushrooms instead of the chicken. Stir-fry them in 2 tbsp of oil and reserve. Cook the noodles in vegetable stock and proceed as above.

Quesadillas

Time: 20 minutes | Makes: 8 quesadillas

Ingredients
- 8 tortillas or rotis
- Oil for cooking

Filling
- 1 tbsp oil
- 1 tbsp finely chopped garlic
- 1 cup red kidney beans (rajma) cooked
- 2 cups finely chopped assorted vegetables (onions, cabbage, beans, carrots, green bell pepper, baby corn, sweet corn, green peas, mushrooms, spring onions)
- 1 tbsp red chilli flakes
- Salt to taste
- ½ cup sour cream (optional)
- ½ cup grated Cheddar cheese

Method
- Put the oil in a pan on medium heat. When hot, add the garlic and sauté, till fragrant.
- Add the kidney beans and heat through.
- Stir in the vegetables and sauté for 3 minutes.
- Add the chilli flakes and salt to taste.
- Place a tortilla or roti on a plate, top with the filling in the centre, allowing space all around the edges.
- Spread 1 tbsp of sour cream over the vegetables, if you like and sprinkle with grated cheese.
- Moisten the edges of the roti with a little water and cover with another roti. Press the edges together.
- Make the remaining quesadillas in the same way.

- Put a tava or griddle on medium heat and spread a little oil over it.
- Put a stuffed quesadilla on it. Roast both sides by flipping over once the base is nicely browned.
- Ensure that you cook it on medium heat, you want the cheese to melt inside.
- Repeat with the remaining quesadillas.
- Remove to a serving plate, slice them into quarters and serve with tomato sauce.

Root Spinach Soup From The Asitane Restaurant

We landed in Istanbul on a cold rainy day and rushed straight into a whirlwind tour of the spice market. The warm aromas and colours, however, were inadequate to keep the fingers of cold from getting through. This soup, at the Asitane restaurant, was a warming welcome to my first taste of Turkish cuisine.

Time: 45 minutes | Serves: 4-6

Ingredients

- 600 gms tender spinach with stalks and roots
- 3 tbsp olive oil
- 1 medium-sized onion, sliced in rings
- ¾ tsp salt
- ½ tsp freshly ground black pepper
- 4 tbsp rice, washed and drained
- 2 eggs, whisked1 tbsp yoghurt, whisked smooth
- 1½ tbsp refined flour (maida)
- 2 tsp lime juice

Method

- Wash the roots, stems and very tender leaves in several changes of water. Drain and break the longer stems and roots into 2-3 pieces. Reserve.
- Put the oil in a large, heavy-bottomed pan on medium heat. When hot, add the onion and sauté, till translucent.
- Add the spinach, salt, pepper and 1½ cups of hot water. Bring to a boil on high heat.
- Add the rice and boil for another 5 minutes.
- Beat the eggs, yoghurt, flour and lime juice together in a small bowl.
- Mix in 3 tbsp of the cooking broth to temper it.
- Slowly drizzle the tempered mixture into the soup.
- Cook, till the rice is tender and serve hot.

Savia Aunty's Signature Figgy Baked Custard

Savia Aunty is my mother's closest college friend. Their friendship has survived more than 30 years, spanning distances, both their marriages, parenthood and many other milestones. Thanks to Savia Aunty, my Mother was introduced to baking and our childhood was enriched with the aromas of Goan food, baked goodies like Easter marzipan and Christmas cake, things that the traditional Gujarati kitchen would never have had. We had this Figgy Baked Custard at her house when we travelled to Goa for her daughter's wedding.

Time: 1½ hours | Serves: 4-6

Ingredients
- 250g dried figs
- 4 eggs
- 6 tbsp sugar
- 1 can (250 ml) condensed milk
- 3 tbsp cornflour

Method
- Soak the figs in hot water for 4 hours. Drain, cut in half and reserve.
- Beat the eggs with the sugar in a bowl and add it to the condensed milk in the upper pan of a double boiler.
- Place the double boiler on low heat and cook, stirring all the while, to make a thick custard. (Don't let the milk boil or it will curdle.)
- Mix the cornflour with 4 tbsp of water and stir it into the custard. Continue to cook, till thick.
- Pour the custard into a baking dish.
- Gently drop the fig halves into the dish, one at a time.
- Place the baking dish in a tray of water and bake in an oven preheated to 180°C for 45 minutes to 1 hour, till cooked at the centre; a toothpick inserted into the centre should come out clean.

Neha's Chilli Con Carne

This is my youngest sister's recipe for chilli con carne. Have it as a one-dish meal or use it to fill baked potatoes; spoon it over corn chips and top with cheese for nachos; or as a pizza topping.

Time: 25-30 minutes | Serves: 4

Ingredients
- 1 tbsp oil
- 2 medium-sized onions, finely chopped
- 2-3 garlic cloves, crushed
- 1½ tbsp cumin powder
- 1½ tbsp coriander powder
- 2 tsp red chilli powder
- 500 gms lamb, minced
- 400 gms canned Italian tomatoes, diced
- 2 tbsp tomato purée
- 1 cup chicken stock
- 300 gms red kidney beans (rajma), cooked and drained
- 2 tbsp chopped pickled jalapeños,
- 2 spring onion bulbs, finely sliced diagonally
- 3 fresh red chillies, chopped
- Salt and freshly ground black pepper to taste

To serve
- 2 tbsp sour cream
- 8 flour tortillas or rotis

Method
- Put the oil in a non-stick frying pan on medium-high heat. When hot, add the onions and garlic and sauté for 3 minutes, till the onion is soft.
- Add the spice powders and cook, stirring for 1 minute.

- Add the mince and cook, stirring to break up lumps, for 5 minutes, till it changes colour and darkens.
- Stir in the tomatoes, tomato purée, chicken stock and beans. Reduce the heat to medium and simmer, stirring occasionally for 10 minutes, till the mixture thickens.
- Remove from heat and stir in the jalapeños, spring onions and red chillies.
- Season with salt and pepper to taste.
- Top with sour cream and serve with warm tortillas or rotis.

Chinese Chilli Mushroom Pot Rice

Time: 1 hour | Serves: 4

Ingredients
- 3 tbsp peanut oil
- 1" piece of fresh ginger, sliced
- 2 medium-sized onions, cut into wedges
- ½ cup sliced garlic
- 250 gms button mushrooms, sliced
- 50-60 gms spring onion greens, cut into 1" lengths
- 5-6 dried cloud ear mushrooms, soaked
- 4 cups chicken stock
- 1 tsp ginger-garlic paste
- 3 tbsp soy sauce
- 4 tbsp cornflour
- 4 cups rice, half cooked
- 3 tbsp toasted sesame oil
- 2 tbsp chilli oil
- Salt to taste

Method
- Put the peanut oil in a wok on high heat, till smoking. Add the ginger first, then add the onions and garlic. Stir-fry on high heat, till the onions and ginger begin to scorch.
- Add the button mushrooms and continue to stir-fry on high heat, till the mushrooms have brown patches on them and they dry out and shrink. They will also make squeaky sounds.
- Add the spring onion greens, stir briefly and transfer to a bowl. Reserve.
- Drain the cloud ear mushrooms and reserve the soaking liquid.
- Slice the mushrooms and add them to the same wok with their soaking liquid, the stock, ginger-garlic paste and soy sauce. Put the wok on high heat and bring to a boil.

- Dissolve the cornflour in a little water and add it to the boiling stock, stirring vigorously to avoid lumps.
- When the stock begins to thicken, add the sautéed vegetables, rice, sesame oil and chilli oil.
- Taste and add salt if required.
- Stir well, cover and simmer, till the rice is cooked through but there is still a little gravy left in the pan.
- Serve hot.

Pinky's Khow Suey

This is my friend Pinky Chandan Dixit's vegetarian version of the traditional Burmese dish. It is essentially a one-dish meal comprising noodles in a soup of curried vegetables in coconut milk, served with a variety of contrasting accompaniments. Each of your guests can individually mix the rich array of accompaniments to create their own taste sensations.

Time: 1 hour | Serves: 4

Ingredients

- 2 packets (400 gms) egg noodles, boiled

Khow suey

- 1 tbsp + 1 tbsp oil
- 2 medium-sized onions, finely chopped
- 1 tsp finely slivered fresh ginger
- 2 tsp finely chopped garlic
- 1 tsp coriander powder
- 1 tsp cumin powder
- ½ tsp turmeric powder
- 2 tbsp gram flour (besan), roasted
- 2 cloves
- 1" cinnamon stick
- 1 bay leaf
- 2 cans (400 ml) coconut milk
- Juice of ½ a lime
- 1 tsp sugar
- Salt to taste
- 1½ cups chopped assorted vegetables (baby corn, broccoli, carrot, French beans and cauliflower), blanched

Accompaniments

- ¼ cup peanuts, roasted and salted
- ¼ cup sliced spring onions with some of the tender greens
- 4 lime wedge
- ¼ cup sliced onions, deep-fried
- ¼ cup chopped garlic cloves, deep-fried
- 3 fresh red chillies, sliced

Method

- Put 1 tbsp of oil in a pan on medium heat. When hot, sauté the onions, ginger and garlic, till the onions are soft.
- Add the spice powders and mix well, till fragrant.
- Remove and purée the cooked mixture in a blender.
- Add the roasted gram flour and blend again. Reserve.
- Put 1 tbsp of oil in the same pan on medium heat. When hot, add the cloves, cinnamon and bay leaf.
- Stir in the puréed paste and coconut milk and bring to a boil.
- When it comes to a boil add the lime juice, sugar and salt and remove from heat.
- Add the boiled vegetables just before serving and heat through.
- To serve, divide the noodles into soup bowls and pour the hot broth over. Serve with all the accompaniments in small bowls alongside.

A Perfect Bite

Ever since I can remember, when I eat, I need to get all the elements on my plate perfectly balanced in each bite. Not only am I obsessed with getting the perfect bite, it is a hobby to create a perfect bite of an ingredient.

And then one day, after a cooking class I conducted, I came home with flavours and ingredients bouncing around in my head like spices in a mortar and pestle. And not just with food combinations but recipes I had to make and cravings that woke me up moments after going to bed. And then I realised, this is what a perfect bite was about. Creating that perfect bite of flavour, texture and taste.

Today my cooking is dictated by seasonal produce from different markets in Mumbai. It all started when I gave in to a long time desire to go exploring Mumbai's markets with my friend and fellow food writer Vikram Doctor. Vikram is very much a market enthusiast and an advocate of food foraging albeit in a uniquely Mumbai way — he goes to specific places to buy specific things. In fact he has it down to a fine art. I am just learning!

Both of my grandmothers shopped at Bhajji Gali, a market walking distance from their homes and one that I had grown up visiting. But it took Vikram to truly open my eyes to the treasures it held, such as the elusive Moras Bhajji, a leafy green found here occasionally. Thanks to Vikram, over time I have discovered a whole new aspect of Mumbai. From Bhajji Gali to the south Indian dominated Matunga market, to the source of everything, Crawford market. I still shop at the supermarket close to me if I am desperate but I shop at local markets whenever possible.

Every market trip yields some new ingredient and adds to the adventure of finding new things to cook with. It also sometimes presents challenges, like getting innovative with decidedly uninspiring ingredients such as cabbage, yam and jackfruit. But I have managed tasty dishes with each of those too. And all said and done, it increased my repertoire of dishes and made me quite adept at varying menus based on available ingredients. In doing this I returned to a tradition that is ancient in India, shopping fresh and local — after all, meals in India are defined by a visit to the local market!

I do not believe I need to know how to cook something before I buy it. Okay, so cooking something new can be scary, but vegetables are cheap (and still are, relative to other ingredients) and buying a small amount of what looks good won't set me back that much. As for what to do with it … well I can figure that out later. The vendors I buy from usually prove to be a font of information, but failing that, research usually yields a few interesting things to try as well. After all we are extremely proficient at using Google to help us figure things out, right? And I have found that being clueless about an ingredient can sometimes lead to the most delicious results.

Curry Leaf Fish

Time: 20 minutes | Serves: 2

Ingredients
- 4 (100 gms each) fish fillets
- 10-12 spicy Thai green chillies
- 30 garlic cloves, finely chopped
- 1 cup curry leaves, finely chopped
- 1 tsp salt
- 1 tbsp oil
- Juice of 1 lime

Method
- Wash the fish and pat dry.
- Combine the green chillies, garlic, curry leaves and salt in a bowl.
- Divide in half and marinate the fish for 10 minutes in one half of the mixture.
- Put the oil in a pan on medium heat. When hot, add the other half of the curry leaf mix and sauté for 2-3 minutes, till the garlic is golden.
- Add the fish and fry on both sides, till cooked through and firm.
- Alternatively, you can bake the fish.
- Mix the fish into the fried herbs and arrange the pieces in a baking dish, cover with foil and bake in an oven preheated to 180ºC for 20 minutes, till the fish is cooked through and flaky. Uncover and bake for a further 5-8 minutes to crisp it up. Squeeze in the lime juice and stir gently.
- Serve with steamed white rice!

Basil-scented Sunny Side Ups

Basil is truly an incredible herb and is a traditional ingredient in Italian, Mediterranean and Thai cuisines; it is also one of the ingredients of the liqueur chartreuse. It is enjoyed for its rich flavour (mildly peppery with a hint of mint and clove), which is best when the leaves are fresh, though dried and frozen leaves are a fine substitute. Herbalists have, for years, recommended basil for digestive complaints.

Time: 10 minutes + overnight to infuse the oil | Serves: 4

Ingredients

Basil-scented oil

- ½ cup rice bran oil
- 2-3 garlic cloves, crushed
- A handful (30 gms) of basil leaves

Sunny side ups

- 4 eggs at room temperature
- 2 tbsp basil-scented oil
- 1 tbsp freshly ground black pepper
- Salt to taste

Method

Basil-scented oil

- Put the oil in a small pan on high heat, till hot but not smoking.
- Add the crushed garlic. Stir and cook for not more than 1 minute, till fragrant.
- Remove from heat and add the basil leaves. Stir well.
- Cover and leave to infuse for at least 1 hour (preferably overnight).
- When cool, strain into oil spritzer bottle.

Sunny side ups

- Warm a non-stick frying pan on low heat. Place a pancake ring on the pan.
- Spray the pan and ring with a little basil-scented oil.
- Crack 1 egg carefully inside the ring. It will sizzle as it hits the pan.
- Use a fork or toothpick to burst any bubbles that might form in the egg.
- Once the egg white has solidified, remove the pancake ring.
- Cook the egg according to your preference (soft/medium/hard).
- Sprinkle with salt and pepper to taste.
- Serve.

Tip: For a different flavour, use any fresh and intensely aromatic herb instead of basil leaves in the oil.

Vikram's Ambadi Dal

'It's a simple recipe,' he shot off to me over the phone one day. 'It's wonderful, rich tasting, yet refreshing and very healthy.' Which is probably why it has stuck with me. I love to fortify lentils and pulses with leafy greens. In this recipe, Vikram combines husked, split moong, dry-roasted to increase its earthy taste, with the thick leaves of Malabar spinach (mayalu/besale/pui-shaak) for its slightly sticky gelatinous texture, roselle leaves for a sour lift and finishes with a panch-phoran tadka in ghee.

Time: 40 minutes | Serves: 4

Ingredients
- 1 cup husked, split moong beans (moong dal)
- 100 gms Malabar spinach
- 100 gms roselle leaves (ambadi)
- ½ tsp salt

Tempering
- 2 tbsp ghee
- 1 tbsp panch phoran
- ½ tsp turmeric powder

Method
- Wash the dal in several changes of water, till the water runs clear. Drain thoroughly and dry completely under a fan.
- Wash the spinach and roselle leaves thoroughly in several changes of water. Drain.
- Roast the dal in a heavy-bottomed frying pan on medium heat, tossing all the while, till it turns golden brown and nutty.
- Transfer to a pressure cooker with the spinach, roselle leaves, salt and 4 cups of water. Pressure-cook for 10 minutes on low heat, after the cooker reaches full pressure.

- Remove from heat and set aside, till the pressure subsides.
- Open the cooker and adjust the consistency of the dal to your taste, adding hot water as needed and mix well.
- Put the dal on medium heat and boil for about 7 minutes.
- Put the ghee for the tempering in a small pan on medium heat. Add the panch phoran and wait till it crackles.
- Add the turmeric powder, carefully so it does not burn and immediately pour the tempering over the dal.
- Serve hot with steamed white rice and lime wedges on the side.

Green Peppercorn Pesto

Green peppercorns are unripe pepper berries that would be dried into black and white pepper if their development were not arrested by early harvesting. I look forward to their arrival with great anticipation and love them for their bright, intense aroma, accented with hints of what I can only describe as 'green'. I pickle a batch every year so I can extend their season for a longer time. (They last for over a year.) And the pickled ones work just as well as the fresh peppers. Their flavour brings a piquant accent to dishes. Try adding ground green peppercorns to creamy sauces or a few bunches of pickled whole ones to a Thai curry at the very end of cooking. This pesto is an ideal vehicle for the peppercorns. Make a batch and stir into hot, freshly cooked pasta, add to white sauce or spoon on to pasta or grilled chicken. It freezes well too.

You can take the short cut and grind the green peppercorns in a blender, using just a few sprigs so you get a coarse texture but I highly recommend pounding this pesto in a mortar and pestle. The results are phenomenal.

Time: 20 minutes | Serves: 4-6

Ingredients

- ½ cup olive oil + extra to cover
- ½ cup fresh green peppercorns
- 1 cup grated Parmigiano Reggiano cheese
- 2-4 garlic cloves, coarsely chopped
- Salt to taste

Method

- Pour the olive oil into a bowl. Place batches of peppercorn in a mortar and pestle and pound into a paste. Transfer to the bowl of olive oil.
- Add the rest of the ingredients and mix well. Taste and adjust salt.
- To store, transfer to a clean dry jar, top with a little additional olive oil and leave in the refrigerator for up to 2 weeks.
- You can also freeze the pesto for up to 3 weeks. Use an ice tray so you do not have to defrost the whole lot when you want to use it.

Papad Nachos With Sour Yoghurt And Fresh Salsa

Here is a healthier version of a favourite party snack I came up with when my local store ran out of nachos.

Time: 30 minutes | Serves: 4

Ingredients

Sour yoghurt
- 2 cups sour yoghurt hung for 2 hours, whisked smooth
- 2 tbsp fresh cream
- Salt to taste

Spicy tomato salsa salad
- ½ cup finely chopped tomatoes
- ½ cup finely chopped onions
- 1 tsp finely chopped green chillies
- 1 tsp finely chopped coriander leaves
- 1½ tbsp lime juice
- ½ tsp red chilli powder
- Salt to taste

Guacamole
- 2 large ripe avocados
- 1 large red onion, finely chopped
- 1 large tomato, finely chopped
- 2 green chillies, finely chopped
- 3 tbsp lime juice
- ¾ cup coriander leaves, finely chopped
- Salt to taste

To assemble
- 8 papads

Method

Sour yoghurt
- Whisk the yoghurt and cream together and press it through a sieve to strain out any solid bits of cream.
- Add salt to taste, mix well and chill.

Spicy tomato salsa
- Combine all the ingredients in a bowl and toss well.

Guacamole
- Cut the avocados in half and remove and discard the seeds.
- Scoop out the flesh and mash it with a fork.
- Mix in the rest of the ingredients.

To assemble
- Using a pair of scissors cut the uncooked papads into triangles like a pizza.
- Place the triangles flat on a plate and microwave on high for 1 minute. Watch it all the while to ensure the papads don't burn.
- Remove, turn over and microwave again for 1 minute.
- Arrange the cooked papads on a platter with bowls of sour yoghurt, salsa and guacamole on the side.

Star Anise-scented Orange Chicken Pot Noodles

One day, after a cooking class I conducted, I came home with flavours and ingredients bouncing around in my head like spices in a mortar and pestle: sesame and lemon, orange and anise, kaffir lime and chorizo, curry leaves and coconut, cocoa nibs and black cardamom, sage and pumpkin, rosemary and bacon ... I was going dizzy! I invented an aromatic spice rub christened the citrus tzar by my friend Nikhil Merchant, and this is what I made with it.

Time: 45 minutes | Serves: 4-6

Ingredients

Citrus tzar spice mix

- 10 spicy dried red chillies
- 5 star anise flowers (badian)
- ½ cup coriander seeds
- 4 tbsp dried orange peel
- 1 tbsp coarse sea salt

Marinade

- 1 tbsp orange zest
- ⅓ cup honey
- 4 tbsp citrus tzar spice mix
- 1 tsp salt

Orange chicken noodles

- 500 gms boneless chicken breasts
- 2 tbsp oil
- 2 cups orange juice
- 2 star anise flowers (badian)
- 1 chicken stock cube
- 1 tbsp cornflour dissolved in 2 tbsp water

- 4 tbsp toasted sesame oil
- 250 gms noodles, cooked

Garnish

- A handful (30 gms) of coriander leaves
- A handful (30 gms) of fresh basil leaves
- 100 gms sliced shallots, fried

Method

Citrus tzar spice mix

- Put a tava or griddle on medium heat. Toast the red chillies and whole spices separately, till aromatic and slightly darkened.
- Combine the toasted ingredients with the sea salt and zest and pulse gently once or twice in a grinder or blender to make a coarse powder.
- Use as much as you need and store the rest in a clean, dry, airtight container.

Orange chicken noodles

- Combine the marinade ingredients in a bowl and mix well.
- Score the chicken breasts with a sharp knife and rub the marinade into it. Set aside to marinate for 30 minutes.
- Put a pan on medium heat and brush with oil. When hot, place the chicken in it and cook for 3-4 minutes, till browned.
- Flip over and cook for 2-3 minutes longer, till brown on the other side as well. Transfer to a plate. Reserve.
- Pour the orange juice into the pan and stir to deglaze it.
- Add the star anise and crumble in the stock cube. Bring to a boil.
- Add the cornflour paste and stir, till the sauce is just starting to thicken.
- Pour in the sesame oil and remove from heat.
- If you are using a clay pot, soak the top and bottom of the pot in water for about 15 minutes. Drain. If you do not have a clay pot, any pan with a tight-fitting lid will also do.
- Put the cooked noodles into the pot.
- Slice the chicken breasts and layer them over the noodles.
- Spread the sauce over the chicken and noodles. (The sauce should be just slightly thicker than water at this point. It will thicken more as it all cooks.)
- Cover and place the pot in the centre of a cool oven or on very low heat.

- Bake for 1 hour or cook on the stove top for 10 minutes.
- Leave it covered, till ready to serve.
- Wash the coriander leaves thoroughly in several changes of water. Drain well and chop fine.
- Sprinkle the herbs and fried shallots over the dish and serve.
- Dig in. Don't expect leftovers!

Tamarind Aubergine

Time: 35 minutes | Serves: 4

Ingredients
- 1 large (250 gms) aubergine (baingan), peeled and cut into chunks
- 2 tbsp + 2 tbsp olive oil
- A handful (30 gms) of curry leaves
- 2 tbsp coriander seeds
- 4-5 garlic cloves, chopped
- 2-4 dried red chillies, broken in half
- 2 small onions, finely sliced
- 2" piece of fresh ginger, julienned
- 2 tbsp tamarind chutney (commercial)
- ½ cup toasted sesame seeds (til)
- Salt to taste

Method
- Put the aubergine chunks in a bowl and toss with 2 tbsp of oil.
- Transfer to a baking tray and spread the pieces in a single layer. Bake in an oven preheated to 180ºC for 25-30 minutes, till crisp and lightly browned.
- Put 2 tbsp of oil in a pan on medium heat. When hot, add the curry leaves, coriander seeds, garlic, red chillies, onions and ginger and sauté, till slightly crisp and brown.
- Transfer to a bowl and add the tamarind chutney and sesame seeds. Mix well and add salt to taste.
- Add the aubergines and toss gently, till well coated.
- Serve warm or cold.

Rainbow Chard Sauté

Rainbow chard or Swiss chard is basically a multi-coloured relative of beetroot that is often referred to as Swiss chard because of its extensive cultivation in Switzerland. It is important to steam or cook chard lightly as the cellular structure and oxalates need to be broken down with cooking to get to all that goodness. But it is also important not to overcook it as you will lose all those wonderful colours.

Time: 20 minutes | Serves: 4

Ingredients

- 200 gms rainbow or ruby chard
- 2 tbsp extra virgin olive oil
- 12 garlic cloves, crushed
- Salt and freshly ground pepper to taste
- Juice of 1 lime

Garnish

- ½ tsp finely grated lime zest
- ½ cup toasted sesame seeds (til)

Method

- Wash the chard and drain. Cut the leaves into 2" ribbons and the stems into 2" pieces.
- Put a large non-stick pan on high heat and add 1 tbsp of oil. When hot, stir in the garlic and stir-fry, till well browned and aromatic.
- Add the chard leaves in large handfuls, allowing each batch to wilt slightly before adding more.
- Season with salt and pepper and cook for about 8 minutes, stirring frequently, till the leaves are softened and most of the liquid has evaporated.
- Transfer to a bowl and reserve.

- Pour the remaining oil into the same pan. Add the chard stems and cook over medium to high heat for about 5 minutes, stirring occasionally, till crisp but tender.
- Stir in the wilted chard leaves, taste and season with salt and pepper.
- Toss with lime juice and transfer to a serving bowl.
- Sprinkle with the lime zest and sesame seeds and serve right away.

Rainbow Chard Dolmades

Time: 1 hour | Serves: 8-12

Ingredients
- 16 chard leaves
- 3 tbsp olive oil + extra for brushing
- 2-4 limes, sliced

Filling
- 100 gms toasted hazelnuts
- 2-3 garlic cloves, minced
- 1-2 limoo omani (see note on page 269) or ½ tbsp dried mango powder (amchur)
- 1 tbsp freshly grated white pepper
- ½ tbsp salt

Method
- Rinse the chard leaves and cut off the stems.
- Use a rolling pin to flatten the rib of the leaves.
- Place the filling ingredients in a blender and process to make a fine paste. Reserve.
- Spread one leaf on your work surface and place about 1 tbsp of the filling on it just above the stem end and spread upwards to cover the leaf. Fold each side of the leaf over the filling and then roll upwards from the stem end to the top of the leaf.
- Repeat with the remaining leaves.
- Put the oil in a large flat pan on medium heat. When hot, lay the sliced limes in one layer at the bottom of the pan.
- Sprinkle in 2 tbsp water.
- Place the dolmades with the leaf tip facing downwards in the pan.
- Brush the tops and sides of the dolmades with extra oil and put the pan on the top shelf of an oven preheated to 180°C. Bake uncovered for 20 minutes.
- Alternatively, arrange the rolls over the lime slices in a large colander placed

over a pan of boiling water and steam for 10 minutes. Weigh the dolmades down by placing a plate on top of them.
- When cooked, set aside to rest for at least 10 minutes before serving. They are much less likely to fall apart this way.
- Serve cold or at room temperature with lime wedges and a drizzle of olive oil alongside feta cheese, garlic pita bread and a light soup.

Note: Limoo omani, also known as kala nimbu, are lemons that are boiled in salt water and then dried till hard and are used in Irani / Persian / Middle Eastern cooking and add a haunting sourness to certain dishes.

A Fine Balance Double-boiled Soup

I love cluster beans as a side dish tempered with carom seeds as well as in a piquant Sindhi curry, but wanted a recipe that allows their delicate, bitter-sweet flavour to come through. So I created this recipe inspired by Chinese double-boiled soups I discovered on a trip to Singapore. Contrary to the logical conclusion, double-boiled does not mean the soup has been cooked twice but actually means the same as the Western culinary term 'double boiling'. Chinese double-boiled soups, also referred to as herbal soups, are consumed to balance the system. The ingredients go into a deep, thick-walled porcelain jar that is covered and placed in a larger pot and half immersed in water. The whole thing is then covered and left to cook on low heat for hours. This method of cooking ensures that the food cooks in its own juices without any loss of moisture, essence or flavour.

Improvise a double boiler, if you don't already have one, with a pressure pan and a smaller bowl.

Time: 1 hour | Serves: 4

Ingredients

- ½ cup fresh dill leaves (sua bhaaji)
- 250 gms white radish, cut to bite-sized chunks
- 250 gms cluster beans (gwar phalli), trimmed and cut to bite-sized pieces
- 6 dried figs, chopped
- 30 garlic cloves, chopped
- 2 tbsp grated fresh ginger
- 4 cups vegetable stock
- 2 tbsp toasted sesame oil
- Juice of 1 lime
- 1 tsp salt

Garnish

- ½ cup finely sliced spring onion bulbs

Method

- Wash the dill leaves in several changes of water. Drain and chop.
- Choose two small pans that can fit into a larger one.
- Put the dill, radish, beans, figs, garlic, ginger and stock in the smaller pans and cover tightly.
- Fill the large pan with water and bring to a boil on high heat.
- Put the smaller pans into it and reduce the heat to the very lowest.
- Cover the larger pan and cook, till the vegetables are tender.
- Leave covered, till you are ready to serve.
- Stir in the sesame oil, lime juice and salt.
- Serve hot garnished with the spring onions.

Rice Paper Rolls With Crab And Fenugreek Stuffing

Baby fenugreek leaves is another ingredient I discovered thanks to Vikram Doctor. Traditionally, they are sautéed with a touch of garlic and chillies into a sweet, slightly crunchy side dish in Gujarati and Maharashtrian cuisines that I love with dal and rice. It is also great in mesclun salads (a gourmet trend abroad) along with alfalfa sprouts and baby lettuce that Trikaya Agriculture produces, but my favourite way is to use it as a stuffing for Vietnamese rice paper rolls.

Time: 45 minutes | Serves: 4-6

Ingredients

- 200 gms baby fenugreek leaves (methi)
- A handful (30 gms) of fresh basil leaves
- A handful (30 gms) of fresh mint leaves
- A handful (30 gms) of fresh coriander leaves
- 1 tbsp oil
- 3-4 garlic cloves, minced
- 1-2 fresh Thai red chillies
- 100 gms crabmeat, cooked
- 2 tbsp toasted sesame oil
- 1 tbsp lime juice
- Salt to taste
- A few lettuce leaves
- 30 gms spring onion bulbs, sliced
- 10 sheets rice paper

Method

- Wash all the leaves thoroughly in several changes of water. Drain well.
- Put the oil in a pan on medium heat. When hot, add the garlic and red chillies and sauté, till golden.

- Add the crabmeat, sauté for 30 seconds.
- Mix in the fenugreek leaves and stir-fry on high heat quickly to combine and cook, till just wilted but with a crunch. Remove from heat and set aside to cool.
- Stir in the sesame oil, lime juice and salt to taste. Toss well.
- Cut the lettuce, basil, mint leaves, coriander leaves and spring onions using the chiffonade technique. (Stack the leaves with the larger ones at the bottom, roll tightly and slice fine. They will open up into lovely strips.) Mix well and reserve.

To assemble
- Pour about 2 cups of boiling hot water into a shallow bowl.
- Take a sheet of rice paper in your hands and quickly dip it completely into the hot water. Do not soak it, just dip and remove.
- Lay it flat on a glass or ceramic plate.
- Line a little of the lettuce mix along the bottom edge of the sheet, slightly off centre.
- Top with a little fenugreek filling.
- Gently but firmly pack the filling together and fold the bottom edge over it. Fold the left and right sides over the filling.
- Roll up and lay in a platter as you go.
- Serve with a sweet chilli dipping sauce.

Sesame Sprouts With Glass Noodles

Inspired by the Vietnamese glass noodle salad, this fragrant, addictive salad with sprouted sesame is delicious. Sesame sprouts are one of my most delicious discoveries. And they are easy to do too! Simply take a cup of unhusked sesame seeds and soak, till swollen. Drain, dry well by rubbing gently with kitchen paper. Place a dry sheet of kitchen paper in a casserole or airtight Tupperware container and transfer the sesame seeds to that. Spread out thinly, close the container tightly and leave for a few hours. Then put the container in the refrigerator overnight. You will see that they have sprouted the next morning.

Time: 30 minutes | Serves: 4-6

Ingredients

Dressing

- 1 green chilli, finely sliced
- 2 tbsp toasted sesame oil
- 1 tbsp chilli oil
- 1 tsp lime juice
- Salt and pepper to taste

Salad

- 200 gms moong bean sprouts
- 6 cups any stock
- 1 packet (330 gms) dried moong bean or glass noodles
- ½ cup sesame seed sprouts
- 1 head (100 gms) iceberg lettuce, finely shredded

Garnish

- ½ cup toasted sesame seeds (til)

Method

- Combine the dressing ingredients and toss well to mix. Reserve.
- Peel the moong bean sprouts and remove and discard the tails.
- Put the stock in a pan on high heat and bring to a boil. Reduce to a simmer.
- Holding the entire mass of noodles with one hand, dip half into the hot stock, till softened.
- Using clean kitchen scissors cut 3"- 4" lengths and allow to drop into the stock. Repeat with remaining mass of noodles.
- Cook the noodles for 2-4 minutes, till plump and glassy. Drain in a colander; rinse once with cold water and place in large mixing bowl.
- Add the dressing, mix well and leave to chill in the refrigerator.
- When ready to serve add the sprouts and lettuce and toss well again.
- Garnish with the toasted sesame seeds and serve.

Figs With Sharp Cheddar And Spicy Caramel Sauce

Fresh figs come into season in the winter and this spicy-sweet-salty marriage of flavours is the perfect way to serve them. The inspired touch of adding a crushed fresh green chilli was an impulse, but it offset the sweet juicy figs, salty cheese and caramel flavours, leaving a lingering aftertaste with a pleasant back-of-the-throat warmth!

Time: 20 minutes | Serves: 2

Ingredients
Caramel sauce

- 1 cup sugar
- 6 tbsp butter
- ½ cup heavy cream

To assemble

- 4 tbsp caramel sauce
- 1 green chilli, puréed
- 6 fresh plump figs, halved
- 2 tbsp sharp cheddar cheese shavings

Method
Caramel sauce

- Measure all the ingredients and have them ready at the outset.
- Put the sugar in a large, deep, heavy-bottomed pan on medium to high heat.
- When the sugar melts, reduce heat to low, as it can burn very fast. Stir continuously, so that it browns evenly.
- Once the sugar is a rich amber colour, add the butter and mix well, till the butter melts and is absorbed.
- Remove the pan from the heat and slowly add the cream, whisking all the while, till the sauce is smooth and velvety.
- Allow the sauce to cool in the pan, then pour it into glass jars.

- Store in the refrigerator for up to 2 weeks. Warm before serving.
- Use as a topping for desserts, ice creams or even drizzle it over cakes and cupcakes.

To assemble
- Warm the caramel sauce in a pan.
- Stir in the green chilli paste and mix well.
- Spoon 1 tbsp each on to 2 individual dessert plates.
- Arrange three figs on each plate.
- Sprinkle with cheddar flakes. Drizzle with the remaining sauce and serve.

Uma's Rosemary Or Thyme Custard

I met Uma Iyer thanks to the food forums on the website anothersubcontinent.com. We have stayed friends ever since and call each other from wherever we might be, to share the discovery of new recipes and flavour combinations. This is one recipe that made it into my repertoire thanks to those conversations.

Time: 1 hour | Serves: 4

Ingredients
- 1 cup milk
- 1 cup heavy cream
- ⅔ cup + ⅓ cup sugar
- 2 sprigs of rosemary about
- 5"- 6" long or a small handful of thyme sprigs
- ½ packet (5 gms) agar agar
- 1 tbsp cornflour

Method
- Combine the milk, cream and ⅔ cup of sugar in a pan.
- Bruise the rosemary or thyme sprigs with a mallet to crush them lightly.
- Add the herbs to the milk mixture in the pan and bring to a simmer on medium heat.
- Remove from the heat, cover and let the infused milk steep for 1 hour.
- Strain the milk. Squeeze out any remaining liquid from the herbs, then discard them.
- Place the remaining ⅓ cup of sugar in a kadhai on medium heat. Do not stir. When the sugar starts melting, lower the heat and let the sugar caramelise.
- Pour the caramelised sugar evenly into the bottom of a glass dish. Tilt the dish back and forth so that the bottom is evenly coated with the caramel.
- Allow the caramel to cool.
- Pour ¾ cup of the herbed milk with the agar into a pan on medium heat. Bring

to a boil. Add the cornflour to the remaining milk and stir, till smooth.
- Pour this slowly into the boiling milk, stirring all the while.
- Keep stirring, till the custard thickens.
- Pour the custard over the caramel in the dish and let it cool.
- Refrigerate, till cold and set.
- Invert the dish on to a platter and serve.

Multigrain Mix

This recipe came into being as a happy quirk of fate. Post a kitchen cupboard cleanup, I found myself with lots of small amounts of grain that had been set aside because the portions were too small to make an individual serving. Now I usually don't cook grains together because every grain has variable cooking times, but I got wondering what would happen if I did. I realised I had really missed something because I ended up with a grain mix that was textured, colourful and filling. I couldn't help thinking of the millions of ways I might be able to use this mix. It could be sweetened for breakfast porridges; tossed into a quick salad for lunch or a hearty soup for dinner; stir-fried with vegetables, as a fried rice; used as a bed for grilled chicken; or sautéed with jaggery or sugar and nuts into a grain version of meethe chaval … the possibilities were endless!

I have evolved the recipe over time, but it is not written in stone. If you don't have one of the ingredients on hand don't fret, simply substitute more of whatever you do have — rice, millet, whatever. Sometimes I might roast the various ingredients individually before I toss them into the pan, which adds a new dimension to the dish or sauté a few spices in ghee, add the grains, give them a quick stir to coat them and then cook. Each new way of cooking adds a different element to this wonderful combination so feel free to experiment.

Time: 1 hour | Makes: about 20 servings

Ingredients
- 1 cup mixed unpolished rice (red, brown, wild, even parboiled rice)
- 1 cup barnyard millet (jhangora)
- 1 cup cracked wheat (dalia)
- ½ cup finger millet (ragi)

- ½ cup sorghum (jowar)
- ½ cup pearl millet (bajra)
- ½ cup oats
- ½ cup wheat grains, soaked overnight
- 1½ tbsp salt

Method

- Mix all the grains together, rinse well, drain and place in a large, heavy-bottomed pan of 5-litre capacity. Stir in the salt.
- Pour in water to come about 2" over the contents of the pan.
- Put the pan on high heat and bring to a boil.
- Reduce the heat to the lowest and simmer uncovered for 30-40 minutes, till all the water is absorbed.
- Alternatively, pressure-cook with water to cover for 30 minutes on low heat, after the cooker reaches full pressure. Remove from heat and cool.
- Freeze the cooked grain in small portions and use as required.

Note: If you end up with too much water once the grains are cooked, strain off the extra nutrient-rich water and use it to make a clear soup seasoned with pepper, ginger and garlic.

Drumstick And Curry Leaf Soup

One monsoon day I was left with little to cook dinner with, but by a stroke of luck, or perhaps because the food gods were looking after me, what could have been a miserable dinner turned into an adventure as I decided to make something from nothing. The result is this drumstick and curry leaf soup; peppery hot to combat the wet day and soothing in an infinitely delicious way that only a soup can be. All the aromatic, delicious flavour of the curry leaf trapped in a bowl!

Time: 30 minutes | Serves: 2-4

Ingredients

Drumstick stock

- 4 drumsticks, cut into 2" pieces
- 1 small onion, finely chopped
- 1 small carrot, finely chopped
- 5 garlic cloves
- 1" piece of fresh ginger, grated

Soup

- 2 tbsp cold-pressed sesame oil
- 1 dried red chilli, roasted and ground
- ½ tsp whole black peppercorns, roasted and ground
- A handful (30 gms) of curry leaves, finely chopped
- 1 cup curry leaves, puréed with a little water
- Salt to taste
- 50 gms vermicelli, fried

Method

- Combine all the ingredients for the drumstick stock in a pressure cooker with 6 cups of water and pressure-cook for 10-15 minutes on low heat, after the cooker reaches full pressure.

- Remove from heat and set aside, till the pressure subsides. The stock should be mushy.
- Squeeze and strain the contents thoroughly through a strainer. Discard the residue and reserve the stock.
- Put the oil in a deep pan on medium heat. Add the red chilli and pepper. Stir-fry for a minute or so, till fragrant.
- Add the chopped curry leaves and allow to crackle.
- Add the puréed curry leaves and cook for 3-4 minutes, till it comes to a boil and is aromatic.
- Add the drumstick stock and bring to a boil.
- Add salt to taste.
- Top with fried vermicelli and serve hot.

Sprout Salad

Most markets in Mumbai will have a couple of vendors that specialise in sprouts of all kinds from moong beans to chickpeas and matki to vaal beans. These make convenient options to pick up and quickly cook at home. I often get a mix of sprouts that I use uncooked or lightly steamed to make this quick snack or side salad.

Time: 30 minutes | Serves: 4-6

Ingredients
- 1 cup Bengal gram sprouts
- 1 cup moong bean sprouts
- ½ cup fenugreek seed sprouts or baby fenugreek (methi; optional)
- ½ cup finely chopped coriander leaves
- 1-2 green chillies, finely chopped
- 2 small onions, finely chopped
- 1 large tomato, finely chopped
- 1 large cucumber, finely chopped
- 1 large potato, cooked and finely chopped
- 1 tsp salt
- ½ tsp red chilli powder
- Juice of 1 lime
- 2 cups popped grains (sorghum/jowar, finger millet/ragi, wheat)

Method
- Combine everything in a large bowl except the popped grains.
- Mix well, taste and adjust seasoning.
- Add the popped grains at the table. Toss well and serve.

Kuch Meetha Ho Jaaye

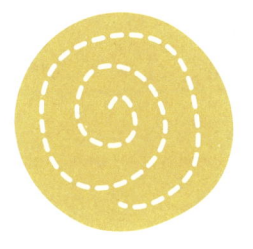

In a culture where sweets hold so much importance I am a bit of a misfit. You see, I have never been a dessert person. For the longest time, till I married, my repertoire of sweets could be counted on one hand. This of course made me a prime candidate of the opposites-attract rule! I married a man with a huge sweet tooth from a family of even bigger sweet lovers! If dessert is my last priority, it is my mother-in-law's first. She will make her dessert and put it aside before she focuses on the rest of any special meal!

'Mithai' means something sweet, or meetha. Meetha is part of the six tastes (or rasas) of Ayurvedic diet: sweet, sour, salty, bitter, pungent and astringent and is considered as important to the health as the other tastes in striking a balance in the diet. Meetha or mithais encompass a phenomenal variety of sweet offerings from the elaborate, often labour-intensive mithais sourced from the local sweet shops to the simpler fresh homemade Laddus, Kheers and Halwas.

Whatever is offered, sweetening the mouth is a quintessential tradition that the women in the house carry forward. From the simple misri (rock crystal sugar) a housewife caught out by a surprise guest will offer, to the dahi-chinni or gur channa they profer to someone leaving for an important task, sweets are symbolic of auspiciousness and good fortune. They are also symbolic of love. There will always be some form of mithai to offer family members and guests alike—usually secreted away from little hands.

Maghas Laddu
(Gram Flour Fudge)

In the Gujarati community, these confections are symbolic of a grandmother's love: the process of making them is long and tiring, so they are made for someone who is very treasured. Maghas (literally meaning brain) is a combination of coarsely ground gram flour mixed with milk and ghee that is considered good for the brain. Family lore says that two or three of these walnut-sized treats washed down with a glass of milk are enough to fill the stomach. Young mothers are advised to feed picky children a couple of these a day.

Time: 20 minutes | Makes: 24 laddus

Ingredients
- 2 cups gram flour (besan)
- 1 tbsp + 1¼ cups ghee
- ½ cup milk, + a few tbsp for moistening
- 2¼ cups powdered sugar
- ½ tsp green cardamom powder

Method
- Place the gram flour in a large thali or platter of 2-kg capacity.
- Using your hands rub about 1 tbsp of ghee into the gram flour.
- Add ½ cup of milk, mix well and leave to rest for 30 minutes.
- Knead the dough, till it reaches the consistency of uniform crumbs — this is called maghas.
- Heat the remaining ghee in a large kadhai or pan of 2-kg capacity. Add the maghas and fry on medium to low heat, till it cooks to a golden-brown colour.
- Remove from heat and allow it to cool slightly, till it is hot but can be handled.
- Add the sugar and cardamom powder and mix while still warm.
- Shape into balls with palms moistened with milk. Store in an airtight container after they are completely cool, till ready to consume.

Shobha's Tilache Laddu
(Sesame Fudge)

Shobha, my Maharashtrian housekeeper, loves making these as much as my kids love to eat them. And I have no complaints because these are incredibly good for them. Use 'chikki cha gud' that you will find at your local grocer. It makes the laddus softer and less brittle when cooked. Use regular jaggery if this is not available.

Time: 2 hours | Makes: 75-100 pieces

Ingredients
- 1 cup white sesame seeds
- ½ cup raw peanuts
- ¼ cup ghee + extra for greasing
- 1 cup grated jaggery
- ¼ cup husked, split, roasted Bengal gram (bhuna chana)
- ½ tsp green cardamom powder

Method
- Roast the sesame seeds and peanuts separately on medium heat, till golden and fragrant. Set aside to cool.
- Once the peanuts are cold, skin them and crush into large bits.
- Put the ghee in a pan on medium heat. When hot, add the jaggery, it will melt and begin to froth.
- Remove the pan from the heat when the jaggery has melted completely.
- Add the sesame seeds, crushed peanuts, gram and cardamom powder. Stir well.
- When the mixture is cool enough to handle, but still warm, coat your hands with a little ghee and shape the mixture into 1" balls.
- Cool completely and store in an airtight container.

Shobha's Lal Tandlach Pithache Ukdiche Modak
(Red Rice Flour Dumplings)

Sweets make perfect offerings and each of the Hindu gods in our pantheon have favourites. The most famous of these divine addictions is that of the genial Lord Ganesha to the modak, steamed pyramids of dough stuffed with coconut and sugar.

Time: 30 minutes to 1 hour | Makes: 6-8 modaks

Ingredients

Filling

- ½ cup grated jaggery
- 1 tsp ghee
- 1 cup grated fresh coconut
- 1 tbsp green cardamom powder

Dough

- 1½ tbsp ghee
- ½ cup red or white rice flour
- A pinch of salt

Method

Filling

- Put a pan on medium heat and add the jaggery.
- When the jaggery starts melting add the ghee and the coconut.
- Mix well and cook on medium heat for 5-6 minutes, till the mixture is sticky and moist.
- Stir in the cardamom powder and remove from heat.
- Set aside to cool.

Dough

- Bring ½ cup of water to a boil in a pan on high heat. Add the ghee.
- Add the rice flour to the boiling water and mix well, stirring continuously.

- Add the salt and cook covered for 2-3 minutes.
- Remove from heat and knead well into a soft dough while it is still hot. Tough as it is, this method is called ukad and is what gives the dish its distinctive flavour, texture and the name.

To assemble and cook the modaks

- Divide the dough into small balls and roll each into discs the size of small puris.
- Place a disc on your palm and put some filling in the centre. Bring the edges of the dough together in pleats as you would for a Chinese dumpling. Form it into a tip at the top and seal by pinching it together.
- Repeat for the rest of the modaks.
- Place the modaks in a steamer or a pressure cooker (without the weight) and steam for 15-20 minutes.
- Serve hot modaks with ghee to Ganeshji first and then indulge!

Rose And Pistachio Labneh Balls Aka Rose And Pistachio Shrikhand With A Twist

A sweet take on the Middle Eastern labneh balls. Labneh are traditionally savoury but I found that the process of making them was similar to our srikhand, where hung yoghurt is sweetened with sugar. So I blended these two recipes to make shrikhand labneh balls.

Time: 10 minutes + 24 hours hanging time for yoghurt | Makes: 30-40

Ingredients
- 2 kg yoghurt
- ½ cup pistachios, flaked
- ⅓ cup rosebud tea or dried rose petals
- ½ tsp coarsely crushed green cardamom
- ⅓ tsp fennel seeds (saunf), toasted and crushed coarsely
- ⅓ cup honey + extra to drizzle

Method
- Spread a thin clean muslin cloth in a strainer placed over a bowl and spoon the yoghurt into it.
- Pull the corners together and tie them together. Suspend this bundle from a stationary object over a bowl or tie it to a rack in your refrigerator with a bowl underneath (to catch the liquid). Allow to hang for about 2-4 hours. What you should aim for is yoghurt the consistency of Ricotta cheese.
- Then put the bundle with the yoghurt in a strainer placed over an empty bowl and leave it in the refrigerator overnight. The next day what you have is labneh.
- Transfer the yoghurt to a bowl and stir in half the pistachios and rosebud tea rose petals and all the cardamom and fennel.
- Combine the remaining pistachios and rose petals in a small saucer and flatten into a thin layer.
- Take about 1 tbsp of the yoghurt at a time and shape into smooth balls.

- Roll them in the pistachio-rose mix and arrange on a tray as you go.
- Drizzle with honey and return to the refrigerator. Chill, till firm.
- When firm, they are ready for consumption. They can also be stored in a clean, dry airtight jar, covered with honey in the refrigerator for up to a week.

Creamy Vanilla-scented Brown Rice Dessert

Here is a tried and tested favourite that I came up with after I discovered the NGO Navdanya. I use all organic ingredients for this. The brown rice breaks down much better than white, giving the pudding a lovely creamy texture without adding cream. The jaggery also lends an earthy sweetness that is more rounded than the sharpness of sugar. This dish does not require too much watching (though you do need to give it an occasional stir). When it is done, put it in a bowl and chill.

Time: 1 hour | Serves: 2-4

Ingredients
- 2 cups brown rice
- 3 cups milk
- ½ cup grated palm jaggery or any other jaggery
- ½ cup seedless raisins
- 1 vanilla pod

Garnish
- A handful of seedless raisins

Method
- Wash the rice and drain it.
- Combine all the ingredients, except the garnish in a medium-sized pan on high heat and bring to a boil.
- Reduce the heat and simmer for 20 minutes, stirring frequently, till the rice has broken down. Remember, it will thicken further as it cools so remove from heat a little before it reaches the consistency you desire.
- Remove the vanilla pod.
- Transfer the custard to a serving dish, garnish with the raisins and serve warm or chilled.
- *Variation: You can substitute vanilla with cinnamon.*

Kiwi Fruit Sandesh

Time: 30 minutes | Makes: 4-8

Ingredients
- 2 firm, ripe kiwi fruits

Filling
- 1 cup fresh cottage cheese (paneer), crumbled
- 4 tbsp sugar, powdered
- 2 green cardamom pods, powdered and strained
- 4 tbsp fresh cream
- 2 tbsp cold milk

Garnish
- 3 tbsp pistachio slivers

Method
- Peel the kiwi fruits and cut each into 4 slices.
- Combine all the ingredients for the filling in a blender and blend well on a low setting.
- Spread the filling over one slice of kiwi fruit and sandwich with another. Press well.
- Decorate with pistachio slivers.
- Repeat with all slices.
- Serve.

Rajma Puran Poli

Many years ago I had Chinese pao or bao in Singapore. Called buns, but more like thick pancakes, they were made of dough and steamed and came stuffed with a variety of fillings. One that I never forgot was stuffed with a thick sweet paste that was elusively familiar. I was told it was a red bean filling. These red beans, called aduki, are similar to rajma, which explained why I found it familiar. While I tasted the familiarity of the rajma the sweetness had my taste buds confounded. I remember thinking at the time that it was such a weird combination to add sugar to a dal but then I was reminded of puran. Puran is a sweet filling in Marathi and poli is flatbread. I have always been fond of these subtly sweet rotis, and I was struck by the similarity between them and the red bean pao/bao. Both are stuffed breads in which the filling consists of a sweet dal paste. So I had an interesting thought: why not try stuffing puran polis with red bean paste instead of the traditional puran for Holi this year? It worked like a charm. And I couldn't help thinking how both the dal pastes made these stuffed breads so much healthier as sweet options for kids.

Time: 1 hour | Serves: 4-6

Ingredients

Red bean paste
- 1 cup small red kidney beans (rajma), cooked till soft but firm
- ½ cup packed dark brown sugar or grated jaggery
- 1 tbsp ghee

Dough
- 1½ cups refined flour (maida)
- Salt to taste
- A few drops of oil + extra for rolling
- Ghee for frying

Method

Red bean paste

- Drain the cooked beans thoroughly and process in a food processor, till smooth.
- Add the sugar or jaggery and process, till just combined.
- Warm the ghee in a pan on medium heat and add the bean paste.
- Cook the mixture, till it is dry and leaves the sides of the pan.
- Remove from heat and store in a covered container in the refrigerator, till ready to use. (It should keep for a week.)

Dough

- Sift the flour and salt into a mixing bowl. Add a few drops of oil and rub with your fingertips, till the mixture resembles breadcrumbs.
- Add up to 2 cups of water, a little at a time and mix to make a loose dough. Cover and set aside for 1 hour.

To make the puran poli

- Pinch off a lemon-sized ball of dough and spread it into a disc with your hands.
- Place a walnut-sized ball of dal mixture in the centre. Bring the edges of the dough over the filling and seal together. Shape into a ball again.
- Apply oil to a plastic sheet and put the stuffed ball on it. Roll it out like a paratha. (The plastic and oil prevents it from sticking.)
- Spread a little ghee on a tava placed on medium to low heat. When hot, lay the poli on it. Cook, till the base is golden brown and small brown patches appear on the surface. Turn over and cook the other side.
- Make all the poli in the same way.
- Serve hot with ghee.

Gujiya / Ghugra
(Star Anise, Orange and Pistachio Puffs)

An exotic version of the Mawa Gujiya my ma-in-law makes every Holi.

Time: 2 hours | Makes: 50-70 pieces

Ingredients

Filling
- 500 gms khoya/mawa (unsweetened milk solids), crumbled
- 200 gms pistachios, toasted and powdered
- 4 star anise flowers (badian), toasted and powdered
- 200 gms castor sugar
- 1 tsp orange zest
- 1 tbsp orange marmalade
- 100 gms ghee

Dough
- 1 kg refined flour (maida)
- 100 gms ghee

Sugar syrup
- 1 kg sugar
- 2 cups orange juice
- 3 star anise flowers (badian)
- 1 tsp orange zest

To cook the gujiyas
- 2 cups ghee

Garnish
- 2 tbsp pistachios, slivered

Method

Filling
- Combine all the filling ingredients in a large pan and mix well.
- Put the pan on low heat and roast, till the sugar dissolves and the mixture is slightly moist. Reserve.

Dough
- Sift the flour into a bowl and mix in the ghee.
- Add up to 2 cups of water, a little at a time and mix to make a soft dough.

Sugar syrup
- Combine all the syrup ingredients in a deep pan and mix well.
- Put the pan on medium heat and cook, stirring frequently, till the sugar dissolves and the syrup is thick.
- Remove and keep warm.

To make the gujiyas
- Divide the dough into lemon-sized balls and roll each ball into a small 4" round roti.
- Put about 1 tbsp of filling in the centre of a roti, ensuring that the edges are free of filling.
- Moisten the edges of the roti and fold one side over the other to form a half moon. Press the edges gently so that they stick together.
- Repeat with the rest of the rotis.
- Put 2 cups of ghee in a kadhai or wok on medium heat. When hot, fry the gujiyas, in batches, if necessary, till golden brown on both sides.
- Drain and place in a tray.
- Pour hot syrup over the gujiyas and allow the excess to drain away.
- Sprinkle the gujiyas with pistachios.
- Cool completely and store in an airtight container.

Sue Darlow's Gajar Halwa

This recipe is a dedication to my friend, the late Sue Darlow, who I met through the food forums at www.anothersubcontinent.com. Sue was a brilliant photographer, friend and colleague who supported me when I just started out as a food writer. She lived in Italy but always connected when she visited India. On one of her trips, when my son Aman was a baby, we made this halwa together and he loved it. It is the first dessert I ever made and it is still a favourite with both my kids.

Time: 1 hour | Serves: 6

Ingredients

- 500 gms carrots, finely grated
- 1 can (400 gms) sweetened condensed milk
- ½ cup fresh milk
- Seeds of 8 green cardamom pods, finely powdered
- 2 tbsp home-made ghee

Garnish

- 2 sheets silver leaf (varq; optional)

Method

- Put the carrots, condensed milk and fresh milk in a pressure cooker, mix well, cover and pressure-cook for about 30 minutes on low heat, after the cooker reaches full pressure.
- Remove from heat and set aside, till the pressure subsides.
- Open the cooker and add the cardamom seeds and ghee. Keep stirring on low heat, till all the liquid has dried up, and then some!
- Remove and transfer to a serving bowl, decorate with silver leaf when cool, if desired.

Lavender Pepper Vodka Thandai

Time: 20 minutes + overnight for soaking | Serves: 8-10

Ingredients
- 3 tbsp poppy seeds
- 125 gms almond flakes
- 3 tbsp whole white peppercorns
- 4 tbsp lavender flowers
- 1 ½ litres milk
- 1 small can (250 gms) condensed milk
- 1½ cups vodka

Method
- Soak the poppy seeds in water overnight.
- Drain and grind the poppy seeds with the almonds, pepper and lavender to make a fine powder.
- Heat the milk in a large pan and add the condensed milk and the powdered spices. Simmer for 15 minutes on medium to low heat.
- Remove, cool and then chill in the refrigerator.
- When ready to serve, stir in the vodka.
- Alternatively, you could steep all the crushed spices in the vodka for 3-4 days.
- Combine the milk with the condensed milk in a pan, boil and chill.
- Stir in the flavoured vodka and serve.

Pomegranate Chocolate Mousse

Time: 45 minutes | Serves: 6

Ingredients
- 2 cups heavy cream
- 1 cup chopped dark chocolate or ready chocolate chips
- 100 gms butter
- ½ cup pomegranate molasses (see note below)

Garnish
- 2 tbsp cocoa powder

Method
- Put the chocolate or chocolate chips in a bowl with the butter.
- Put the cream in a pan and place it on medium heat, just till it comes to a boil.
- Pour the hot cream over the chocolate and butter and whisk gently, till the chocolate and butter melt completely and it forms a smooth glossy ganache.
- Stir in the pomegranate molasses.
- Pour the mousse into a flat, glass dish, so that it comes less than halfway up the dish.
- Dust with cocoa powder.
- Chill.

Note: *Pomegranate molasses is a staple in Middle Eastern cooking. It is used in marinades, rubs, or glazes and even desserts. To make it, combine 4 cups of pomegranate juice, 1 tbsp sugar and ½ tbsp lime juice in a pan and bring to a boil on medium heat. Simmer for 45 minutes to 1 hour, till it thickens to the consistency of thick molasses. Transfer to an airtight container and store in the refrigerator for up to a month.*

In Gratitude (My personal Oscar speech)

I have always believed that I am the person I am because of people around me who have invested time, effort and love in me. Here, at this moment in time, I have reached a turning point in my life — written a book! In a sense this has perhaps been longer and tougher to do than giving birth. Future books will come, but none will be the first, so this is most definitely the time to say, 'Thank You'.

~ In memory of: Moti Mummy, Hamir Munshaw, R D Ghildiyal, Hasit Munshaw and Ashutosh Munshaw

~ Dedicated to:~ Nirmala Mulraj, the most happening nani in the world! ~ my mothers, Heena Munshaw and Saroj Ghildiyal, in every way I couldn't be without you two.~ my best friend, Chandra Shekhar Ghildiyal

When I was young, I spent hours fantasising about the man I would fall in love with. Mom often told me that real life was very different and there was nothing like a Prince Charming. She was right. No fantasy of Prince Charming, knights in shining armour, or anything else my mind ever conjured up can match reality. Reality is much better because you are real and very, very imperfectly, perfect for me... The curve of your neck is made for me to tuck my face into and your hands are made to cup my head and settle it there. You are my greatest strength and my biggest weakness. Not only do you fix everything around the house and in my life (my hero!), you hold fort when I go off on wild adventures, being father and mother to our kids and take on the world for me. You have been my haven through tough times but what you do not know is that when great happiness comes, when my work is rewarded, you are the one I want to share it with. You are the one that celebrates ME with me. Like that diamond you are going to buy me one day needs the right setting to sparkle, I needed you to realise my full potential. This book is as much yours as it is mine. Looking forward to the many fabulous meals we will cook in our café together under that mango tree in DD. Now if only you'd learn to READ a recipe!

~ my beautiful children, Aman and Natasha Ghildiyal who made me a mother and my adorable nephews Ishaan Munshaw and Nirvaan Bajaj, my niece Alisha Luhar and all the future grand-children of the Munshaw family. Ever since Aman opened his eyes and looked up at me that first time, I have wanted to leave him, and later all of you, something to be proud of. All of you come from very, very special roots and I cannot think of anything better than this, a small idea of where you come from, to give you.

- to my siblings, Kunal (even though you will always be rude about what I serve you, nothing can beat all the delicious FLY [insect] soups you served me. Eh Dicoo? Love you, Hate you — wouldn't trade you for the world!), Himanshi and Neha, who know me and love me in spite of it. And to their spouses, Sheetal, Vishal and Mohit, who chose to marry Munshaws, survived it and made us all the better for it (LOL).

- to Vipul Binjola, because words cannot describe what you mean to me.

- Aditya Heble and Archana Heble, my 'go to' people.

- to my teachers Mrs Dias, Mehta Sir, Dr R.S. Wagh, Dipika Hazra and MOST, MOST especially to Anahita Lee, for nurturing me and believing in me.

- to the many friends, foodie and otherwise, that have helped me along the way, knowingly or unknowingly.

- Ashutosh Pathak who should know why he is here without my having to put it in words ...

- Roshan Tamang for every single ROSS Moment I have had over the years — thanks for listening all those years ago and introducing me to blogging even though it was just to get me out of your chatbox so you could work! Oh and for the momo recipe! And for cheering me on always!

~ Mrigank Sharma, who came into my life as a food photographer and stayed to become one of my closest friends. Thank you for giving me this week from your life to translate my ideas into visuals so beautifully (and for shaving on the last day so I could get that behind-the-scenes picture of you!). You are a special person and I am glad we are friends!

~ Priya Coulagi, Mita Iyer, Pinky Chandan Dixit, Uma Iyer, Karishma Pais and Saee Koranne Khandekar, Rhea and Kurush Dalal and Lalita Iyer for inspiring me, each in their own way as well as for their infallible support as surrogate moms, babysitters, sounding boards, voices of caution and most importantly for always encouraging every bizarre endeavour I embark on!

~ Bishwanath Ghosh who saw me through the toughest part of writing this book.

~ Arnab Chakladar and the founding team of 'Another Subcontinent'. Sanjeev Kapoor for being a cooking inspiration, Antoine Lewis and Vikram Doctor for guiding and inspiring me, Rajeev Matta, Monika Bhide, Suvir Saran, Mohit Khattar, Vikas Khanna, each of whom has played a part in who I am today —thank you!

~ And lastly, thank you also to Deepthi Talwar who has patiently seen me through this book and to Preeti Singh, who took on the task of editing this book— my mother will thank you for presenting her absentminded daughter to the world better! Thank you all!

Index of Recipes

BEVERAGES

Cutting chai *page 4*

Lavender pepper vodka thandai *page 299*

Moti Mummy's chai masala house blend *page 2*

Munshaw house chai *page 3*

Rose and pistachio kehwa *page 6*

Nani's special chaas (Buttermilk) *page 52*

Suleimani chai *page 5*

BREADS

Methi thepla (Fenugreek-flavoured flatbread) *page 25*

Nani's milk bread *page 29*

CHUTNEYS, SAUCES & DIPS

Green peppercorn pesto *page 258*

Kairi ni chutney (Green mango chutney) *page 63*

Kumi bhabhi-inspired hearty Mexican bean dip *page 139*

Mayonnaise *page 127*

Spice of life *page 56*

Sun-dried tomato sauce *page 149*

Thencha-inspired pesto *page 201*

Tomato chutney *page 158*

Tomato sauce *page 220*

White sauce *page 64*

White wine sauce *page 166*

Zhanzhanit Maharashtrian mirchi thencha (Pounded chilli chutney) *page 202*

DAIRY- & COCONUT-BASED DISHES

Cheese soup *page 64*

Chilli cheese melts *page 136*

Coconut curry *page 98*

Kiwi fruit sandesh *page 293*

Rose and pistachio labneh balls aka rose and pistachio shrikhand with a twist *page 290*

DESSERTS & SWEETS

Aam papad (Mango leather) *page 9*
Chocolate hazelnut spread *page 184*
Copra pak (Coconut fudge) *page 31*
Creamy vanilla-scented brown rice dessert *page 292*
Figs with sharp Cheddar and spicy caramel sauce *page 276*
Fruit pizza *page 186*
Gujiya/ghugra (Star anise, orange and pistachio puffs) *page 296*
Maghas laddu (Gram flour fudge) *page 286*
Marble cake with raisins and cherries *page 134*
Mohanthal (Gram flour fudge) *page 100*
Morio (Spicy, savoury yoghurt and millet porridge) *page 12*
Nani's date cake *page 30*
Neha's twist on Mayo cake: chocolate balls *page 126*
Phirni (Rice custard) *page 86*
Pinky's carrot cake *page 197*
Pomegranate chocolate mousse *page 300*
Rajma puran poli *page 294*
Rose and pistachio cake *page 168*
Savia Aunty's signature figgy baked custard *page 243*
Shobha's lal tandlach pithache ukdiche modak (Red rice flour dumplings) *page 288*
Shobha's tilache laddu (Sesame fudge) *page 287*
Sue Darlow's gajar halwa *page 298*
Tapkhir jo halvo (Arrowroot fudge) *page 44*
Uma's rosemary or thyme custard *page 278*

EGGS

Basil-scented sunny side ups *page 254*
Green garlic and coriander frittata with tomato chutney *page 158*
Zarine's Parsi papeta per eeda (Eggs over potatoes) *page 212*

LENTILS, PULSES & LEGUMES

Non-Vegetarian
Maghas laddu (Gram flour fudge) *page 286*
Neha's chilli con carne *page 244*

Rajma puran poli *page 294*
South African bunny chow recipe à la Rushina *page 232*

Vegetarian
Amiri khaman (Bengal gram snack) *page 79*
Dal kababs *page 143*
Fada ni khichdi (Moong and broken wheat medley) *page 106*
Fada no sheero (Broken wheat dessert) *page 108*
Sev tameta nu shaak (Gram flour string and tomato curry) *page 104*
Gujarati dal dhokli (Lentils with wheat flour dumplings) *page 93*
Handvo (Gujarati cuisine's answer to meatloaf) *page 10*
Khatta dhokla (Spicy sour buttermilk steamed cakes) *page 50*
Ivy gourd moong dal salad *page 81*
Khatta moong (Spicy whole moong bean and yoghurt soup) *page 60*
Kumi Bhabhi-inspired hearty Mexican bean dip *page 139*
Lachko or kathan dal (Thick, tempered lentils) *page 45*
Lobia (Black-eyed beans) *page 118*
Lonavala baked beans *page 236*
Masoor dal (Husked, split Egyptian lentils) *page 114*
Methi dal dhokli (Lentils with fenugreek-stuffed wheat flour dumplings) *page 95*
My Le Crueset bean cassoulet *page 164*
Neelu Bhabhi's chole bhature *page 140*
Osaman (Spicy thin lentil soup) *page 46*
Pratima Foi's dakkho (A slowly simmered vegetable stew enriched with pulses and legumes) *page 88*
Sesame sprouts with glass noodles *page 274*
Sindhi curry (Piquant tomato and gram flour curry) *page 206*
Sprout salad *page 284*
Usha's maa ki dal (Slow-simmered black gram) *page 214*
Vikram's ambadi dal *page 256*
Winnie Aunty's sprout salad *page 205*
Yasmin's Bohri chana bateta *page 208*

MEAT
Chicken
Chicken Mexican wrap *page 180*

Mayo chicken curry *page 122*
Pho (Vietnamese noodle soup with chicken) *page 238*
South African bunny chow recipe à la Rushina *page 232*
Star anise-scented orange chicken pot noodles *page 262*

Mutton & Lamb
Bourbon and rosemary mutton potato pie *page 174*
Clove-scented lamb in red wine *page 170*
Kacchhe kheeme ke kabab (Minced mutton kababs) *page 222*
Keema pasta *page 112*
Kofta curry *page 116*
Mayo mutton curry *page 120*
Neha's chilli con carne *page 244*
Ross' momos or pot stickers *page 220*

Pork
Lora's Goan sausage pulao *page 210*

Seafood
Curry leaf fish *page 253*
Kalyan's doi posto eelish (Hilsa in a poppy seed and yoghurt gravy) *page 218*
My sister Himanshi's prawn curry *page 228*
Nairobi butter tava prawns *page 84*
Rice paper rolls with crab and fenugreek stuffing *page 272*
Sheetal's prawn curry in green masala *page 230*

MISCELLANEOUS GRAINS
Multigrain mix *page 280*
Sama sabudana dhokla (Sanwa millet and sago cakes) *page 34*

PASTA & NOODLES
Non-Vegetarian
Best spaghetti and meatballs ever! *page 194*
Keema lasagne *page 160*
Keema pasta *page 112*
Pho (Vietnamese noodle soup with chicken) *page 238*

Star anise-scented orange chicken pot noodles *page 262*

Vegetarian
13-onion pasta *page 130*
Broccoli and cauliflower pasta *page 188*
Garlic noodles / pasta alio olio and pasta alio olio e pepperoncino *page 150*
Hakka noodles *page 74*
Pasta from scratch with white wine sauce *page 166*
Pinky's khow suey *page 248*
Spaghetti in spinach sauce (Worms in monster blood for some!) *page 182*
Sun-dried tomato pasta *page 149*

PICKLES & PRESERVES
Chundo (Spicy mango pickle) *page 40*
Haldar nu athanu (Fresh turmeric pickle) *page 14*
Leeli mari nu athanu (Green peppercorn pickle) *page 16*
Methambo (Mango pickle) *page 42*
Mixed vegetable pickle *page 18*
Murrabba (Mango preserve) *page 15*

RICE
Non-Vegetarian
Cindy's porridge or congee *page 237*
Hainanese chicken rice *page 234*
Lora's Goan sausage pulao *page 210*

Vegetarian
Chinese chilli mushroom pot rice *page 246*
Creamy vanilla-scented brown rice dessert *page 292*
Fried rice *page 71*
Idli *page 192*
Mushroom dum biryani *page 146*
Phirni (Rice custard) *page 86*
Rainbow idlis *page 192*
Shobha's lal tandlach pithache ukdiche modak (Red rice flour dumplings) *page 288*

SALADS & RELISHES

Cabbage yoghurt salad *page 163*
Ivy gourd moong dal salad *page 81*
Khamang kakdi (Coconut cucumber salad) *page 24*
Mexican potato salad *page 227*
Mom's house salad *page 66*
Root and shoot salad *page 152*
Sesame sprouts with glass noodles *page 274*
Sprout salad *page 284*
Week's worth salad *page 154*
Winnie Aunty's sprout salad *page 205*

SNACKS

Non-Vegetarian

Kacchhe kheeme ke kabab (Minced mutton kababs) *page 222*
Ross' momos or pot stickers *page 220*

Vegetarian

Chilli cheese melts *page 136*
Cornflake chivda (Cornflake snack) *page 101*
Dakor na gota (Spicy gram flour fritters) *page 82*
Dal kababs *page 143*
Handvo (Gujarati cuisine's answer to meatloaf) *page 10*
Khara ané mitha chavda or pudla (Sweet and spicy crêpes) *page 32*
Mohanthal (Gram flour fudge) *page 100*
Morio (Spicy, savoury yoghurt and millet porridge) *page 12*
Pattice (Coriander-stuffed potato fritters) *page 36*
Sama sabudana dhokla (Sanwa millet and sago cakes) *page 34*
Sesame potato footballs page 183Trail mix treasures *page 187*
Tapkhir khandvi (Spiced buttermilk squares or rolls) *page 38*
Trikona puri (Triangular deep-fried puffed flatbreads) *page 105*
Vatana na ghugra (Green pea fritters) *page 102*

SOUPS

Non-Vegetarian

Thukpa or gya thuk in Tibetan (Noodle soup) *page 223*

Vegetarian

Buttered vegetables and clear soup *page 198*
Carrot and onion soup with parsley oil *page 128*
Dal soup (Tempered lentil soup) *page 58*
Drumstick and curry leaf soup *page 282*
Gujarati kadhi (Spicy yoghurt soup) *page 19*
Khatta moong (Spicy whole moong bean and yoghurt soup) *page 60*
Railway tomato soup *page 119*
Roasted pumpkin soup with spiced cointreau butter, candied orange zest *page 172*
Root spinach soup from the Asitane Restaurant *page 242*
Spinach soup *page 78*
Sweet corn soup *page 69*

SPICE PASTES & POWDERS
North Indian daag curry base *page 144*

VEGETABLES
Aubergines
Aubergine in sweet-sour sauce with spring onions *page 70*
Tamarind aubergine *page 265*

Avocado
Papad nachos with sour yoghurt and fresh salsa *page 260*

Broccoli
Broccoli and cauliflower pasta *page 188*

Cabbage
Cabbage yoghurt salad *page 163*

Carrot
Carrot and onion soup with parsley oil *page 128*

Cauliflower
Broccoli and cauliflower pasta *page 188*

Cauliflower or okra tempura *page 67*
Sesame cauliflower *page 190*

Corn
Makai ni khichdi (Spicy corn curry) *page 97*

Cucumber
Khamang kakdi (Coconut cucumber salad) *page 24*

Drumsticks
Drumstick and curry leaf soup *page 282*

Gourds
Dudhi nu shaak (Bottle gourd stew) *page 55*
Ivy gourd moong dal salad *page 81*
Roasted pumpkin soup with spiced cointreau butter, candied orange zest *page 172*
Turiya shaak (Ridged gourd stew) *page 62*

Green Peas
Vatana na ghugra (Green pea fritters) *page 102*

Leafy Greens
Methi dal dhokli (Lentils with fenugreek-stuffed wheat flour dumplings) *page 95*
Rainbow chard dolmades *page 268*
Rainbow chard sauté *page 266*
Root and shoot salad page *152*
Root spinach soup from the Asitane Restaurant *page 242*
Sesame potato footballs *page 183*
Spaghetti in spinach sauce (Worms in monster blood for some!) *page 182*
Spinach soup *page 78*
Vikram's ambadi dal *page 256*

Mixed Vegetables
13-onion pasta (A fine balance double-boiled soup) *page 130*
Cindy's porridge or congee *page 237*

Spicy layered vegetable casserole *page 132*
Mom's house salad *page 66*
Pinky's khow suey *page 248*
Pratima Foi's dakkho (A slowly simmered vegetable stew enriched with pulses and legumes) *page 88*
Quesadillas *page 240*
Sambhariye jo shaak (Stuffed mixed vegetables) *page 48*
Sweet and sour vegetables *page 72*
Undhiyu (Winter vegetable medley in green spices) *page 20*

Mushrooms
Mushroom and potato gratin *page 157*
Mushroom dum biryani *page 146*

Okra
Cauliflower or okra tempura *page 67*

Onions
Carrot and onion soup with parsley oil *page 128*

Potatoes
Aloo chenchki (Nigella-scented potatoes) *page 216*
Mexican potato salad *page 227*
Pattice (Coriander-stuffed potato fritters) *page 36*
Schezwan potatoes *page 68*
Sesame potato footballs *page 183*
Spicy potato pinwheels *page 124*
Thencha potatoes *page 204*
Yasmin's Bohri chana bateta *page 208*

Tomatoes
Sev tameta nu shaak (Gram flour string and tomato curry) *page 104*
Railway tomato soup *page 119*
Sindhi curry (Piquant tomato and gram flour curry) *page 206*
Sun-dried tomato pasta *page 149*

WHEAT

Bhature *page 140*
Fada ni khichdi (Moong and broken wheat medley) *page 106*
Fada no sheero (Broken wheat dessert) *page 108*
Gujarati dal dhokli (Lentils with wheat flour dumplings) *page 93*
Puran poli (Sweet, lentil-stuffed griddle breads) *page 294*
Trikona puri (Triangular deep-fried puffed flatbreads) *page 105*